MANAGING CAPITAL RESOURCES FOR CENTRAL CITY REVITALIZATION

CONTEMPORARY URBAN AFFAIRS
VOLUME 7
GARLAND REFERENCE LIBRARY OF SOCIAL SCIENCE
VOLUME 1205

Managing Capital Resources for Central City Revitalization

edited by
Fritz W. Wagner
Timothy E. Joder
and
Anthony J. Mumphrey, Jr.

HT
175
.M37
2000
West

The Maxine
Goodman Levin
College of
Urban Affairs at
Cleveland State
University

Garland Publishing, Inc.
A member of the Taylor & Francis Group
New York and London
2000

Published in 2000 by
Garland Publishing, Inc.
A member of the Taylor & Francis Group
19 Union Square West
New York, NY 10003

10   9   8   7   6   5   4   3   2   1

Library of Congress Cataloging-in-Publication Data
Managing capital resources for central city revitalization / edited by
    Fritz W. Wagner, Timothy E. Joder & Anthony J. Mumphrey, Jr.
        p.   cm. — (Garland reference library of social science ; v.
    1205. Contemporary urban affairs ; v. 7)
        Includes bibliographical references.
        ISBN 0-8153-3213-0 (alk. paper)
        1. Urban renewal—United States.   2. Urban cores—United States.
    3. Central business districts—United States.   4. Urban policy—
    United States.   I. Wagner, Fritz W.   II. Joder, Timothy E.
    III. Mumphrey, Anthony J.   IV. Series: Garland reference library of
    social science ; v. 1205.   V. Series: Garland reference library of
    social science.   Contemporary urban affairs ; v. 7.
    HT175.M37   1999
    307.3'416—dc 21   99-26782
                                                                      CIP

Printed on acid-free, 250-year-life paper.
Manufactured in the United States of America.

Contents

Acknowledgments   vii

Series Editor's Preface   ix

Chapter 1 Managing Capital Resources   1
Robert W. Becker and Robert A. Collins

Chapter 2 Impacts of Urban Redevelopment in
Central City Neighborhoods   19
Michael Goodman and Daniel Monti

Chapter 3 TOADS: Instruments of Urban Revitalization   45
Elise Bright

Chapter 4 Managing Development in New York City:
The Case of Business Improvement Districts   81
Edward T. Rogowsky and Jill Simone Gross

Chapter 5 Sports Stadia: A Strategy for
Downtown Redevelopment   117
Arthur C. Nelson

Chapter 6 Conclusion: Summary and Future Research   147
Fritz W. Wagner, Timothy E. Joder,
and Anthony J. Mumphrey Jr.

v

About the Editors 155

About the Contributors 157

Index 161

Acknowledgments

This book and its companion volume, *Human Capital Investment for Central City Revitalization*, are the products of a two-year endeavor by the National Center for the Revitalization of Central Cities. The National Center is a consortium of academic institutions that analyzes critical problems facing America's central cities, evaluates strategies to address those problems, and recommends policy alternatives.

The idea for the National Center was borne in 1991 as part of an urban development seminar series. Louisiana's former senior senator, J. Bennett Johnston, turned this academic discussion into a tool for research and policy-making. Senator Johnston sponsored the National Center in the U.S. Congress. Because of its initial success (1992–1994), the National Center was refunded—in the amount of one million dollars—to pursue an ambitious agenda. If not for J. Bennett Johnston and strong support from New Orleans' mayor, Marc Morial, the National Center would not have continued its work. This book, *Managing Capital Resources for Central City Revitalization*, is one product of their commitment to urban policy and research, and to the nation's investment in central cities.

We also recognize our National Center colleagues at Boston University (Michael Goodman and Daniel Monti), the University of Texas at Arlington (Richard Cole and Elise Bright), City University of New York (Ronald Berkman, Edward Rogowsky, and Jill Gross), and the Georgia Institute of Technology (Arthur C. Nelson). Their research and analyses for the National Center have made significant contributions to the urban planning/urban development literature.

We also appreciate the work of many other people who were instrumental in this effort. Arthur Nelson helped write the book proposal that we submitted to Garland Publishing. Richard Bingham, series editor of Garland's Urban Affairs collection, recognized the important contribution our research could make to the urban affairs/urban studies discipline in selecting this manuscript for publication. Kristi Long and Becca MacLaren, the social science editorial staff at Garland, showed great patience as we struggled to put each chapter together. Robert Becker, vice president of planning and operations for the New Orleans Audubon Institute and an adjunct professor at the College of Urban and Public Affairs, University of New Orleans, reviewed drafts of each chapter and agreed to cowrite the introduction. Robert Collins, a doctoral candidate in the urban studies program at the College of Urban and Public Affairs, provided an overview of the urban development literature. Lauren Schrantz, publications coordinator for the college, formatted each research study into a working paper and then consolidated them into a single manuscript. And last but not least, Krishna Akundi brought the final product to fruition, coordinating the assembly of our colleagues' work and acting as our interface with the publisher.

Our sincere thanks to all.

Fritz W. Wagner
Timothy E. Joder
Anthony J. Mumphrey Jr.

February, 1999
University of New Orleans
New Orleans, Louisiana

Series Editor's Preface

Managing Capital Resources for Central City Revitalization is the first of two books in the Contemporary Urban Affairs series stemming from research conducted by the National Center for the Revitalization of Central Cities. In this book, a number of urban scholars examine and evaluate various ways in which central cities attempt to stimulate economic growth and development in a postfederal environment. In Chapter 2, for example, a number of different development strategies are examined in terms of their effects on the vitality of the city as a whole, the redeveloped neighborhoods, and adjacent neighborhoods.

But the heart of the book is the detailed examination of three interesting economic development strategies: reusing temporarily obsolete, abandoned, and derelict structures (TOADS), establishing business improvement districts, and siting sports stadia. Drawing from the commonalities of the case studies, the book concludes that, in the current postfederal environment, five factors are advisable for successful central city revitalization: developing public–private partnerships; making a commitment to physical revitalization to improve quality of life among central city residents; taking a holistic view of the benefits to the entire region rather than focusing on individual neighborhoods; involving all actors in the planning process; and crafting strategies to take advantage of the unique strengths of each central city.

When a book has chapters authored by different individuals, it is often difficult to ensure that there is an even quality to all of the work. But this is not the case with *Managing Capital Resources for Central*

City Revitalization. The chapters fit well into the editors' framework. The book makes an important contribution to the study of the development of the contemporary city.

Richard D. Bingham

CHAPTER 1

Managing Capital Resources

ROBERT W. BECKER AND ROBERT A. COLLINS

Since the end of World War II, the United States has invested significant physical and financial resources to revitalize central cities. Some federal efforts at revitalization, such as urban renewal, have been piecemeal and haphazard; others, such as the urban development action grant program, have been qualified successes. Since 1980, however, the federal government has significantly diminished its commitment to America's central cities.

Urban mayors and state governments made up for reduced federal funding by offering tax incentives (especially tax-increment finance districts and tax abatements) to attract industry. Through such incentives, many central cities—particularly between 1982 and 1988—rehabilitated major portions of their downtowns with new construction and new investments in commercial, office, and retail uses. The economic recession that began in 1989 and continued through 1992, however, reduced the number and type of tax and other locational incentives that local governments could offer to attract industry.

In contrast to well-known locational incentives, a few locally based revitalization experiments have been all but overlooked in the literature. This is possibly because these initiatives have not been formally supported by the federal government. In this book, the contributors examine how central cities manage their physical and fiscal resources (or capital assets) so that the central city continues to be a center of business and residential activity.

Each chapter in this text shows how central cities meet the goals of economic growth and development in a postfederal environment. As federal and state resources devoted to central cities have declined, and as traditional financing mechanisms prove counterproductive to growth and development, municipalities have designed strategies and programs to manage their capital resources better. These local strategies and programs include the reuse of temporary obsolete abandoned derelict structures; the establishment of business improvement districts; and the construction of sports, convention, and entertainment venues. Better management of capital resources leads to economic growth and development and thus to urban revitalization. Moreover, the strategies presented here reveal that better management of capital resources raises the standard of living for central city residents.

In this introductory chapter, we define terms, give an overview of the urban development literature, and provide an organizational structure for the remainder of the book.

DEFINITION OF TERMS

Managing capital resources for central city revitalization: What do these terms mean? Many textbooks on urban revitalization do not explicitly give operational definitions. The authors of these texts assume that the reader ascribes the same meaning as they do to technical terms. Although reader and author may often agree, we should not leave this apparent consensus to chance. Here, we build on the conceptual framework used by Pagano and Bowman (1995: 21), who describe city efforts at urban revitalization as "mobilizing public capital":

> Public capital . . . denotes not only monetary resources or investments but anything of value, tangible or intangible, available for development purpose. Public capital is the collection of policy instruments that city governments have at their disposal to encourage, control, or complement development. Mobilization refers to the sequential process of selection, packaging, and utilization of those resources.

Thus, the process of managing capital resources for central city revitalization may be operationally defined as the efforts taken by municipalities to utilize their assets (be they physical or monetary, public or private) for the purpose of facilitating economic development in central cities during a period of diminishing federal support.

Examining each phrase more closely, what is meant by "managing capital resources"? In the political economy literature (see Logan and

Molotch 1987), **capital** usually refers to the **exchange value** of local resources. Exchange value may be defined as the rent that accrues to the owners of property. Property is usually associated with land and the structures sited on that land. These structures include festival market- places, convention centers, hotels, stadia, aquariums, museums, water- front developments, office developments, mixed-use developments, luxury housing, and retail centers (Schwartz 1995). In addition, structures also refer to public capital investments: highways, streets, sidewalks, transit systems, sewerage, sanitation, parks and recreation, and public build- ings—including schools, health units and hospitals, and fire and police stations (Gramlich 1994). Property, however, is not limited to real estate; it also takes into account other physical, intellectual, and financial goods and services.

How do public officials effectively and efficiently **manage** capital in- vestment? What are the best means to facilitate **economic development**? Beauregard (1993) characterized economic development as a process in which individuals and organizations engage in the production, distribu- tion, and consumption of goods and services. However, the direct benefits of economic development are confined to those who make the invest- ments (corporate executives, financiers, real estate developers, and indus- try representatives) and their institutional partners (commercial banks, pension funds, venture capital). If these agents of economic development do not reap positive returns (or increasing rents) from their investments at a particular site, they will move to other locations and thus allow that ini- tial site to deteriorate (Feagin 1987; Harvey 1989; Soja 1989; Stone 1987). Discussions on the consequences of capital investment as well as statistical data reveal that, more often than not, that initial site has been the central city. Central cities and their low-income residents suffer from the investment decisions of the corporate and power elite.

It seems ironic that city officials would place the interests of central city residents second to those of capital. But, as described by Sam Bass Warner in *The Private City* (1962), this has been true of our nation since its very beginnings. The relationship between capital and the central city has been described by the concept of **privatism**. Privatism refers to the active role of government in increasing exchange value for the benefit of property owners. Squires (1991: 199–200) defines privatism in this way:

> [C]oncretely, the policies of privatism consist of financial incentives from government (e.g., tax abatements, low interest loans, land write- downs, tax increment finance districts, enterprise zones, urban devel-

opment action grants, industrial revenue bonds, redevelopment author-
ities, and eminent domain) to private economic actors. These financial
incentives are intended to reduce factor costs of production and en-
courage private capital accumulation, thus stimulating investment
which ultimately serves both private and public interests.

These financial incentives—which have historically managed the central
city's capital resources and increased its exchange value—tend not to increase use value (Logan and Molotch 1987). Traditional financial/loca-
tional incentives do not necessarily enhance human activity in the central
city as a place to live, work, and play. Therefore, the goal behind managing capital resources for central city revitalization should be to maintain
the balance between exchange value and use value. The contributors to
this text consider this balance.

What is meant by the phrase "central city revitalization"? The **central city** is commonly known as the core or center of a metropolitan area.
A central city, compared to surrounding municipalities, is also characterized by a greater population density as well as by a greater density of
economic activity (Bogart 1998; Mills 1972). Within the central city,
density of economic activity in the downtown area or central business
district is greater than at other areas in the central city. Downtowns, at the
expense of other central city locations, have experienced considerable
revitalization. According to Holcomb and Beauregard (1981: 1),

> urban revitalization implies growth, progress, and the infusion of new
> activities into stagnant or declining cities which are no longer attrac-
> tive to investors and middle class households. Typically, urban revital-
> ization involves investment to remodel or rebuild part of the urban
> environment to accommodate more profitable activities and expanded
> opportunities for consumption, particularly retail and housing for mid-
> dle- and upper-income households . . . areas of the city are upgraded
> for higher social and economic uses.

The main ideas discussed in this section—exchange value, use
value, and privatism—address a consistent theme found in most of the
urban revitalization literature.

OVERVIEW OF THE URBAN DEVELOPMENT LITERATURE

Our objective is not to classify the exhaustive literature on urban development. Since a logical and orderly national research agenda has been

lacking in this field, much of the available literature has been sporadically reported by researchers from a number of disciplines, including architecture, geography, history, political economy, sociology, and urban planning. Moreover, these scholarly efforts have been uncoordinated. We are concerned with those recent works on urban development that provide a policy-oriented perspective and an evaluative perspective of revitalization strategies.

The historical record (see Chudacoff and Smith 1994) reveals that the problems associated with our central cities have been brewing since the early 1900s but it was not until the 1950s that the urban predicament received wide public attention. Even then—as Teaford (1990) points out—strategies to revitalize the central city have been piecemeal and haphazard. Central cities continue to decline in population, employment, and incomes. The suburbs, on the other hand, prosper. Should federal and state governments frame a coherent policy to revitalize the central city? Peterson (1985) holds that, in the new urban reality, central cities should be allowed to fail; no set of place-based strategies can retard or reverse the social-economic-political decline of the urban core. In contrast, Cisneros (1993) argues that the urban core is the engine that drives the regional economy and thus the national economy. Therefore, Congress and the president must draft a national strategy for revitalizing the central city.

Peterson (1985) and Cisneros (1993) reprise the ongoing policy debates between people-based strategies and place-based strategies. People-based strategies are those policies and tools designed by government (more commonly at the federal level) to enhance use value. Place-based strategies are those policies and tools designed by government (either at the federal, state, or local level) to increase exchange value. It should come as no secret to the student of urban affairs that the nation's revitalization policies have tended toward place-based strategies: urban renewal, urban development action grants, enterprise zones, and the cornucopia of tax incentives. These strategies, however, generally have not benefitted low-income residents of older industrial cities.

In 1985 the Brookings Institution released Paul Peterson's volume, *The New Urban Reality.* Peterson and colleagues contend that the twin issues of technology and race argue against further investments in the central city. They address two main questions: Is the industrial city declining because technological innovation has rendered its infrastructure and land-use patterns out of date and inappropriate for the late twentieth-century economy? Has racial distrust contributed to the decline of industrial cities by accelerating rates of change in both residential choice and employment opportunities?

Technological advancements have transformed the urban economy from one based on blue-collar labor and manufacturing to one based on services and knowledge-intensive industries. This transformation has also led to higher skills requirements. A consequence of these requirements is increasing productivity, which in turn means increasing incomes for workers. Better incomes, however, allow well-to-do families to take advantage of the larger-sized housing opportunities and other amenities available in the suburbs. This circumstance leaves the central city with a majority of the population that cannot meet the education and training requirements of most good-paying jobs. Thus, the poor labor supply and the growing concentration of poverty in the urban core convince firms to leave the core for other locations (e.g., the suburbs, rural areas, other metropolitan areas, or offshore locations). Moreover, public services are often cut back when central city revenues and intergovernmental aid decline. This action aggravates financial disinvestment: banks cite the lack of adequate public investment and the lack of mortgage demand (Adams 1988; Shlay 1989).

The exodus of the middle class has also left the central city fractured and polarized. The urban core is polarized between an elite but small number of upper-income households and a majority of low-income residents—some of whom are elderly, others who are on welfare, and a growing number who are ethnic minorities (black, Hispanic, and Asian). The urban core is fractured because its ethnic groups perceive each other as competitors in the fight over diminishing resources. Peterson, and the contributors to his volume, recommend policies that afford minorities more residential choices. Specifically, Peterson (1985: 29) suggests that medical, welfare, and social services should be relocated from the central city to small towns and rural areas:

> Such a [dispersal] policy will do more than merely shift the racial problem from cities to small towns and the countryside. The intractable nature of black poverty in the United States comes [in part], from its excessive concentration. Dispersion and diffusion can have multiple benefits. The poor and dependent would have greater choice and need not constantly reconnect themselves to bureaucracies with every move. To the extent that many would move away from the central city, the poor would suffer less crime and enjoy greater family stability.

People-based strategies, such as those proposed by Peterson (1985), rely on an altruistic principle: it is society's responsibility to help those who cannot help themselves, and society in the form of government must serve as the safety net of last resort for households and families. This altruistic desire, however, has not created another New Deal or Great Society. It appears, especially since 1980, that the federal government has taken the position that a political or policy-oriented case for revitalizing the central city and reinvesting in its low-income residents must rest not on altruism but on privatism.

Following the 1989–1992 national economic recession, a unique place-based argument for central city revitalization emerged. The National League of Cities (especially work by Ledebur and Barnes 1993, 1997) and the U.S. Department of Housing and Urban Development (in particular the text edited by former secretary Cisneros 1993) reopened the debate on the relationship between central cities and suburbs. They argued that failing cities breed failing suburbs. Moreover, they claimed that the quality of life in the suburbs depends on a strong central city that provides jobs for the region's residents and houses the region's educational and cultural institutions. Thus, unless socioeconomic decay in the urban core is reversed, it will spread to the inner suburbs, outer suburbs, and the metropolitan fringe (Ledebur and Barnes 1993; Savitch et al. 1993; Voith 1992). In order to reverse decline, federal and state governments must increase public investment in the core. While this dependence argument seems appealing, it is not supported by data: suburbs do not rise or fall with respect to socioeconomic conditions in the central city (Mumphrey and Akundi 1998). Other nationwide strategies for stemming decline and revitalizing the core and its adjacent communities include regional governance structures (Gerston and Haas 1995; Orfield 1997) and targeting dynamic industry clusters (Porter 1995).

Judd and Swanstrom (1998), in *City Politics: Private Power and Public Policy,* examine the nature of privatism in the United States. Some scholars have examined specific examples of privatism (Clarence Stone in *Regime Politics: Governing Atlanta*, Stephen Elkin in *City and Regime*, and Scott Cummings in *Business Elites and Urban Development*) and still others have reviewed federal policy (Kaplan, Marshall, and James 1990; Kleinberg 1995; Waste 1998). Judd and Swanstrom critique federally sponsored place-based strategies that have sustained privatism: urban renewal (established in 1949), model cities (1966), community development block grants (1974), urban development action grants (1978), and empowerment zones (1993).

The urban renewal program, the first nationwide effort at central city revitalization, was a success for the monied interests but an utter failure at upgrading the socioeconomic conditions of central city residents and shopkeepers. The urban renewal program, despite its shortcomings, continued for nearly twenty-five years—from 1949 to 1974 (Judd and Swanstrom 1998). This was partly because every mayor and city council in the country made their requests for some portion of the federal largesse.

Corporate interests originally proposed the idea of renewing the central city to members of the U.S. Congress. Before the concerted efforts of financiers and planners—especially groups such as the American Institute of Architects and the Urban Land Institute—urban redevelopment was not considered by Congress (Foard and Fefferman 1966). The federal mandate, as it concerned urban policy, had always been to provide decent, affordable housing. With the 1949 Federal Housing Act, Congress did not move too far from that mandate. Kleinberg (1995: 144) notes, however, that one clause was especially vague: municipalities could spend monies "[to improve] slum areas by providing better housing or community amenities for residents."

Local priorities—dictated, in part, by chambers of commerce—focused on the clearance of deteriorated business districts and blighted residential areas. Thus, beginning with the 1949 Federal Housing Act, urban renewal meant federally funded land clearance. These clearance projects promoted the construction of new office buildings, hotels, theaters, and convention centers in the central business district. Federal funding also provided for the construction of highway overpasses, underpasses, and on-ramps in downtown (Kleinberg 1995). Chudacoff and Smith (1994) estimate that nearly 2.6 million housing units were demolished between 1950 and 1959 in the name of urban renewal.

The economic expansion that began after World War II and continued through the 1950s was a boon to the nation and metropolitan areas. The urban renewal program was particularly important to metropolitan areas in that it held the promise of a centralized corporate complex—that is, the administrative and management activities of the metropolitan area's large companies could locate in the central business district (CBD). A principal consequence of urban renewal, however, was the eradication of some central city neighborhoods, the displacement of families, and the loss of small businesses (Gans 1962). Even more alarming, urban renewal was associated with "negro removal": over three-fourths of the people displaced by urban renewal in its first eight years and two-thirds of those displaced through 1961 were black (Judd and Swanstrom 1998: 190).

A decade later, during the 1960s, the national economy was growing although residential and industrial migration from the central cities to the suburbs began to increase (Bergman and Goldstein 1983). This migration was helped by urban renewal and highway construction. The civil rights movement was in full swing but riots seized many cities, including New York's Harlem (1964), Los Angeles's Watts (1965), Cleveland's Hough (1966), and Detroit's Twelfth Street (1967). This urban predicament accelerated a shift in federal policy that had been underway for some time: the move from physical redevelopment in the central city (i.e., from privatism) to socioeconomic revitalization (i.e., to policies that enhance use value). This paradigmatic shift, however, was short-lived.

Beginning in 1964, several important social programs were initiated, including Head Start, Upward Bound, Food Stamps, and Medicaid; and the Aid to Families with Dependent Children (AFDC) program was further expanded. In 1965, the Johnson administration established the Department of Housing and Urban Development (HUD). One year later, HUD unveiled its most ambitious project—Model Cities. The Model Cities legislation (or the Demonstration Cities and Metropolitan Development Act of 1966) was a federal commitment to the physical and social rehabilitation of central cities.

The Model Cities program, however, was doomed to failure. First, funds were spread too thin. President Lyndon Johnson had originally proposed targeting five cities as recipients of Model Cities funds but, after negotiations with congressional leaders, that target changed to 75 and a year later 150 municipalities called themselves model cities. Second, the program suffered from poor planning. Municipalities had minimal voice in administering local programs. Federal administrators drafted the guidelines and required recipients to meet countless performance standards. Third, overly optimistic promises were made to assure congressional reauthorizations. The Model Cities program, however, provided only modest gains in central city revitalization.

In contrast to the burst of domestic policy-making in the mid-1960s, Lemann (1989) suggests that during the 1970s the federal government had shifted, once again, to a passive role. Given an environment shaped by high inflation and high unemployment, the federal government opted for handing out more monies to local governments. Some of these monies were wasted by cities and some urban programs and their administration were also misguided. This period foreshadowed an end to the federal government's commitment to central cities.

The Comprehensive Employment and Training Act (CETA) in 1973 and the Community Development Block Grant (CDBG) in 1974 were two of the decade's principal programs designed to improve conditions in low- and moderate-income areas of the central city. While CETA was dismantled in the 1980s, CDBG has endured. This block grant program replaced Model Cities, and it garnered bipartisan support especially from members of Congress who represented large cities and suburban districts as well as from those representing states in the South and West (Kleinberg 1995). However, the Community Development Block Grant program was not favorable to the declining cities of the Northeast and Midwest. In addition, the Brookings Institution discovered that "only 29 percent of CDBG monies were spent in neighborhoods that had lower-than-median family incomes" (Judd and Swanstrom 1998: 229). Municipalities were using CDBG monies to improve citywide services and thus benefit all census tracts in the city.

To correct for the abuses of the CDBG program, the Urban Development Action Grant (UDAG) was established. In principle, UDAG targeted federal funds for commercial, industrial, and residential revitalization in distressed cities. These funds were explicitly designed to leverage private investments, thus bringing capital back to disinvested parts of the city. In practice, however, no means test nor geographic restriction was used. Urban Development Action Grants have been used to build festival malls, convention centers, and public infrastructures. They have also been used to repair historic buildings and support neighborhood improvements.

The UDAG program illustrates the beginning of a paradigm shift in urban policy that was taken to the extreme during the 1980s. Vaughn and Sekera (1982: 81) have written:

> The problem of poverty [some policy analysts and government officials have suggested], stems from a lack of physical and financial capital; thus the solution lies in massive infusions of money for large-scale projects. But, this argument ignores the need to develop institutional capacity and human capital for long-run economic growth. Moreover, physical development projects seldom bring local residents into the planning process.

Recession in the early eighties contributed to ending several federal urban programs, including UDAG. Federal aid to local governments fell consequently. Judd and Swanstrom (1998) report that federal tax policy replaced urban programs and policies. Moreover, responsibility for central city revitalization devolved to the states and the municipalities themselves. A decade (1982–1992) had gone by with no national urban development/revitalization program. A number of state governments, however, created enterprise zones. The objective of the enterprise zone program was to subsidize business investment in designated areas of the state.

The most recent urban revitalization program is the empowerment zone. The current administration proposed and Congress funded the empowerment zone program in 1994. Empowerment zones combine place-based strategy (enterprise zones) and people-based strategies (education, job training, and child care). Thus empowerment zones, at least in theory, maintain a balance between exchange value and use value. The lesson learned from Model Cities was also adopted for the empowerment zone program: do not spread resources too thinly. Accordingly, six cities were designated as full empowerment zones and seventy-two were designated as supplemental zones. Judd and Swanstrom (1998) identify an empowerment zone's four basic components: tax incentives, targeted spending, strategic planning, and public-private partnerships.

Clearly, federal action on central city revitalization has diminished with every administration since 1968. In place of policies that enhance the socioeconomic conditions of residents, federal policy has turned to initiatives that lower the costs of doing business in the urban core and thus increase exchange values. Strategies to manage capital resources for urban revitalization must come from the central city itself. Bingham, Hill, White (1990); Wagner, Joder, and Mumphrey (1995); and Imbroscio (1997) evaluate revitalization strategies that husband diminishing public dollars.

Bingham et al. (1990), in their edited volume, *Financing Economic Development*, consider the following questions: Why should the public invest in private sector activities? Does public investment create jobs and economic development for the community? The essays in this volume discuss the efficacy of public sector financing mechanisms, alternative uses of public funds, and private sector financing. Eight specific programs are evaluated: community development corporations, enterprise zones, industrial revenue bonds, research parks, revolving loan funds, tax increment finance districts, and venture capital. The authors come to no definite conclusions, but call for further research.

Wagner et al. (1995), in their edited volume *Urban Revitalization: Policies and Programs*, examine the application and efficacy of specific revitalization programs in seven case cities: Atlanta (enterprise zones), Baltimore (education and job training), Fort Worth (various federally funded projects), Minneapolis (tax increment finance districts), New Orleans (various federally funded projects), New York (urban development action grants and community development block grants), and Portland, Oregon (urban renewal). In the concluding chapter, the editors find that successful revitalization efforts require strong public leadership, intergovernmental cooperation, long-range planning, and human investment. Key impediments to successful revitalization include cuts in federal aid and the state of the national economy and local economies.

Imbroscio (1997), in *Reconstructing City Politics: Alternative Economic Development and Urban Regimes*, explores the benefits to central cities from strategies that provide communities and municipalities with a greater control of economic resources. Imbroscio examines three strategies: entrepreneurial-mercantilist, municipal-enterprise, and community-based.

Given the dimished federal role and the uncertainity of state-supported tax incentives, many central cities have designed their own revitalization strategies. In this volume, our colleagues at the National Center for the Revitalization of Central Cities examine three such strategies that increase the exchange value of the central city. While these strategies appear to further the "private city" at the expense of use value, a closer inspection reveals that locally based strategies attempt to balance exchange values and use values.

ORGANIZATION OF THE BOOK

The following chapters bring successful redevelopment strategies to the reader's attention. These strategies were designed at the local level and their success rests on the partnerships created among the public, private, and nonprofit sectors of that locality. Each chapter has been written for a general audience and addresses conceptual, investment, and institutional factors. In addition, the contributors to this volume offer conclusions and make policy recommendations at the end of their chapters. These conclusions and recommendations are supported by case study research and statistical analysis.

Michael Goodman and Daniel Monti ask a fundamental question in Chapter 2: Which types of development policy improve the socioeconomic conditions of a community? They evaluate the impact of active and supportive development strategies on central city neighborhoods in Atlanta, Minneapolis, New Orleans, and Portland, Oregon. Goodman and Monti define active strategies as those that emphasize the public sector's dominant role in the planning and funding of a development project, such as the Louisiana Superdome. Supportive strategies reveal that the public sector's role is merely to leverage private funds; the private sector plays a larger role in the planning and implementation of the project, as in the case of New Orleans's Downtown Development District.

The development typology provided by Goodman and Monti also classifies the revitalization strategies described by the other authors in this text. In Chapter 3, Elise Bright discusses the reuse of temporarily obsolete abandoned derelict structures (TOADS) as a tool for urban revitalization—this is an example of active development policy. Edward Rogowsky and Jill Gross, in Chapter 4, examine the establishment of business improvement districts (BIDs)—this is an example of supportive development policy. In Chapter 5, Arthur Nelson's study of sports stadia is an example of an active development policy.

Elise Bright reports on the efforts of public–private partnerships in eleven North American cities (including Boston, New York, Pittsburgh, Portland, Providence, and Seattle) to reuse/redevelop TOADS. Specifically, the author shows that these structures—which in the past contributed to neighborhood decline—could be used to improve the quality of life for residents in low-income neighborhoods. TOADS are usually private properties that revert to the local government because of delinquent taxes, abandoned urban renewal projects, abandoned rights-of-way, HUD foreclosures, military base closings, school closings, Resolution Trust Corporation reversions, and other forms of public condemnation.

Rogowsky and Gross explore the role of private investment decisions to direct central city revitalization in Chapter 4. Specifically, they assess the function of business improvement districts (BIDs) to revitalize New York City. These BIDs are special taxing districts formed by property owners according to state criteria. The tax revenues collected in these districts can be used to increase law enforcement, landscaping, street maintenance, and physical rehabilitation in the district. The authors find that, at least in New York City, there are three types of business improvement districts: the corporate BID which is represented by the Metrotech area in downtown Brooklyn; the main street BID, which is represented by the Fulton Mall in downtown Brooklyn and the Jamaica Center in Queens; and the community BID, which is represented by the 165th Street Mall in Queens.

Nelson, in Chapter 5, addresses the following question: If sports stadia come to the metropolitan area, where should they go—the central business district, elsewhere in the central city, or the suburbs? Nelson does not debate the efficacy of luring professional sports as a tool for urban revitalization. Based on a robust statistical analysis of forty-three metropolitan areas, he finds that there is a relationship between stadium location and economic development. This analysis is important because if teams, and therefore stadia, merely displace leisure dollars, the overall health of the economy does not improve. However, if people are drawn to sports facilities and spend money before and after events, there may be significant indirect economic effects. Nelson's results indicate that the closer to the central business district a stadium locates, the larger the positive economic effect on the metropolitan area. The magnitude of that effect, however, depends on the size of the metropolitan area. The larger the metropolitan area, the smaller the economic effect of sports stadia. Conversely, sports stadia have a large economic effect on small and mid-sized metropolitan areas.

In the final chapter, Wagner, Joder, and Mumphrey summarize the principal lessons for managing capital resources: (1) develop public–private partnerships, (2) commit to physical revitalization for improving the quality of life among central city residents, (3) take a holistic view—that is, rehabilitating a neighborhood or urban area should be viewed in terms of its benefits to the region, (4) begin a strategic planning process that involves all actors (government, business, residents)—do not mandate from above, and (5) one size does not fit all—that is, revitalization strategies must be crafted to take advantage of the unique strengths of each central city. The authors also comment on the general direction that urban policies have taken in the last twenty years, and point to areas suitable for future research.

Authors' Note: We would like to thank Fritz Wagner, Tim Joder, and Tony Mumphrey for their comments on previous drafts of this chapter.

REFERENCES

Adams, C. 1988. *The politics of capital investment: The case of Philadelphia.* Albany: State University of New York Press.

Beauregard, R. 1993. Constituting economic development: a theoretical perspective. In *Theories of local economic development.* R. Bingham and R. Mier (eds.). Newbury Park, CA: Sage Publications.

Bergman, E., and H. Goldstein. 1983. Dynamics and structural change in metropolitan economies. *Journal of the American Planning Association.* 49(3): 263–79.

Bingham, R., E. Hill, and S. White, eds. 1990. *Financing economic development: An institutional response.* Thousand Oaks, CA: Sage Publications.

Bogart, W. 1998. *The economics of cities and suburbs.* Saddle River, NJ: Prentice Hall.

Chudacoff, H. and J. Smith. 1994. *The evolution of American urban society.* Englewood Cliffs, NJ: Prentice Hall.

Cisneros, H., ed. 1993. *Interwoven destinies: Cities and nation.* New York: Norton.

Cummings, S., ed. 1988. *Business elites and urban development: Case studies and critical perspectives.* Albany: State University of New York Press.

Elkin, S. 1987. *City and regime in the American republic.* Chicago: University of Chicago Press.

Feagin, J. 1987. *The capitalist city: Global restructuring and community politics.* New York: Oxford University Press.

Foard, A. and H. Fefferman. 1966. Federal urban renewal legislation. In *Urban renewal: The record and the controversy.* Wilson, J. (ed.). Cambridge: M.I.T. Press.

Gans, H. 1962. *The urban villagers: Group and class in the life of Italian Americans.* New York: Free Press.

Gerston, L. and P. Haas. 1995. Political support for regional government in the 1990s: Growing in the suburbs. *The Regionalist,* 1(1): 65–73.

Gramlich, E. 1994. Infrastructure investment: A review essay. *Journal of Economic Literature.* 32: 1176–1196.

Harvey, D. 1989. *The urban experience.* Baltimore: Johns Hopkins University Press.

Holcomb, B. and R. Beauregard. 1981. *Revitalizing Cities.* Washington, DC: Association of American Geographers.

Imbroscio, D. 1997. *Reconstructing city politics: Alternative economic development and urban regimes.* Thousand Oaks, CA: Sage Publications.

Judd, D. and T. Swanstrom. 1998. *City politics: Private power and public policy.* New York: Longman.

Kaplan, Marshall, and Franklin James, eds. 1990. *The future of national urban policy.* Durham: Duke University Press.

Kleinberg, B. 1995. *Urban America in transformation.* Thousand Oaks, CA: Sage Publications.

Ledebur, L. and W. Barnes. 1997. *Local economies: The U.S. common market of local economic regions.* Thousand Oaks, CA: Sage Publications.

Ledebur, L. and W. Barnes. 1993. *All in it together: Cities, suburbs, and region.* Washington, DC: National League of Cities.

Lemann, N. 1989. The unfinished war. *The Atlantic Monthly.* (January): 52–71.

Logan, J. and H. Molotch. 1987. *Urban fortunes: the political economy of place.* Los Angeles: University of California Press.

Mills, E. 1972. *Studies in the structure of the urban economy.* Baltimore: Johns Hopkins University Press.

Mumphrey, A. and K. Akundi. 1998. Suburban dependency hypothesis, reconsidered. *Journal of Planning Literature, 13*(2): 147–157.

Orfield, M. 1997. *Metropolitics: A regional agenda for community stability.* Washington, DC: Brookings Institution.

Pagano, M. and A. Bowman. 1995. *Cityscapes and capital: politics of urban development.* Baltimore: Johns Hopkins University Press.

Peterson, P., ed. 1985. *The new urban reality.* Washington, DC: Brookings Institution.

Porter, M. 1995. The competitive advantage of the inner-city. *Harvard Business Review* (May/June): 55–71.

Savitch, H., D. Collins, D. Sanders, and J. Markham. 1993. Ties that bind: Central cities, suburbs, and the new metropolitan region. *Economic Development Quarterly, 7*(4): 341–357.

Schwartz, A. 1995. Rebuilding downtown: A case study of Minneapolis. In *Urban revitalization: Policies and programs.* F. Wagner, T. Joder, and A. Mumphrey (eds.). Thousand Oaks, CA: Sage Publications.

Shlay, A. 1989. Financing community: methods of assessing residential credit disparities, market barriers, and institutional reinvestment performance in the metropolis. *Journal of Urban Affairs* (Summer): 201–223.

Soja, E. 1989. *Postmodern geographies: The reassertion of space in critical social theory.* London: Verso Press.

Squires, G. 1991. Partnership and the pursuit of the private city. In *Urban life in transition.* M. Gottdiener and C. Pickvance (eds.). Thousand Oaks, CA: Sage Publications.

Stone, C. 1989. Regime politics: Governing Atlanta, 1946–1988. Lawrence, KS: University Press of Kansas.

Stone, C. and H. Sanders, eds. 1987. *The politics of urban development.* Lawrence: University Press of Kansas.

Teaford, J. 1990. *The rough road to renaissance: Urban revitalization in America, 1940–1985.* Baltimore: Johns Hopkins University.

Vaughn, R. and J. Sekera. 1982. Development for whom: a critique of federal development policy. In *Public policies for distressed communities.* S. Redburn and T. Buss (eds.). Lexington, MA: Lexington Books.

Voith, R. 1992. City and suburban growth: Substitutes or compliments? *Business Review, Federal Reserve Bank of Philadelphia.* 21–33.

Wagner, F., T. Joder, and A. Mumphrey, eds. 1995. *Urban revitalization: Policies and programs.* Thousand Oaks, CA: Sage Publications.

Warner, S. 1962. *The private city: Philadelphia in three periods of growth.* Philadelphia: University of Pennsylvania Press.

Waste, R. 1998. *Independent cities: Rethinking U.S. urban policy.* New York: Oxford University Press.

CHAPTER 2

Impacts of Urban Redevelopment in Central City Neighborhoods

MICHAEL GOODMAN AND DANIEL MONTI

Many contemporary analysts of urban redevelopment tend to take a skeptical view of the prospects of urban redevelopment efforts to produce lasting revitalization in American central cities (Squires, 1994). Many of these communities in the United States are argued to be racially and economically segregated (Massey and Denton, 1993). The social problems created by this segregation are said to fall especially hard on low-income minority persons who are arguably becoming increasingly isolated from their more prosperous neighbors (Massey et al., 1994).

The prospect of redeveloping inner-city neighborhoods in a way that brings different classes or races together receives even less favorable reviews. Instead of fostering integration, most redevelopment strategies are often expected to produce gentrified areas where people who are better off find a comfortable place to live or enclaves that provide a refuge for people from the same ethnic group (Beauregard 1985; Cicin-Sain 1980; Palen and Nachmias 1984). Some evidence of neighborhood stabilization efforts driven by private institutions support this contention (Taub et al. 1984). At least one case study of similar redevelopment efforts in St. Louis, Missouri reaches a different conclusion (Monti 1990; Goodman and Monti 1999).

This chapter attempts to describe the impact of a variety of redevelopment strategies on the social and economic vitality of inner-city communities by examining sixteen central city neighborhoods in four large American cities: Atlanta, Georgia; Minneapolis, Minnesota; New Orleans, Louisiana; and Portland, Oregon.

Specifically, this has involved tracking social and demographic change over time (1950–1990) in selected neighborhoods within these cities. The experiences of eight neighborhoods that have been affected by redevelopment projects are compared to those of eight adjacent neighborhoods that remain free of substantial redevelopment activities.

METHODOLOGY

Revitalization Strategies

A wide variety of revitalization strategies has been employed by the four cities examined over the course of the past fifty years. Frequently, individual cities employ multiple strategies in their inner-city redevelopment efforts. Therefore, it is very difficult to assess the efficacy of particular revitalization strategies. However, when the entire range of strategies is closely examined, two fundamental strategic orientations become apparent. Individual redevelopment efforts can be effectively characterized as involving either active or supportive strategic orientations to inner-city redevelopment.

Active revitalization strategies emphasize a strong public-sector role in both the planning and funding of central city redevelopment projects. These strategies make substantial use of local, state, and federal funds to implement publicly developed revitalization plans.

In contrast, supportive revitalization strategies involve a different public sector role in the development process. While frequently making use of public funds, these types of strategies emphasize leveraging private funds for redevelopment activities and encouraging business and community involvement in the planning and implementation of redevelopment projects and revitalization efforts.

We examine four neighborhoods (one from each city) that have been redeveloped "actively" and four neighborhoods (one from each city) that have been "supportively" redeveloped. The social and demographic experiences of these eight neighborhoods are then systematically compared with the experiences of adjacent areas which have remained free of substantial redevelopment efforts. These comparisons allow a comprehensive description of the social and economic consequences of these two major public meta-revitalization strategies (see Table 2–1).

The Neighborhoods

This chapter revisits a series of case studies of redevelopment undertaken by a number of scholars affiliated with the National Center for the Revi-

Table 2–1
Actively Developed Neighborhoods and Adjacent Areas

City	Neighborhood	Redevelopment Project
Atlanta GA	Vine City	World Congress Center
Atlanta GA	EnglishAvenue	Not substantially redeveloped
Minneapolis MN	Downtown West	Hennepin County Government Center
Minneapolis MN	Downtown East	Not substantially redeveloped
Portland OR	Downtown West	The Transit Mall/MAX
Portland OR	Downtown East	Not substantially redeveloped
New Orleans LA	Central City North	The Superdome
New Orleans LA	Central City South	Not substantially redeveloped

Supportively Developed Neighborhoods and Adjacent Areas

City	Neighborhood	Redevelopment Project
Atlanta GA	Summerhill	Underground Atlanta
Atlanta GA	Atlanta University	Not substantially redeveloped
Portland OR	Lloyd District	Convention Center
Portland OR	Goose Hollow	Not substantially redeveloped
Minneapolis MN	Loring Park	Loring Park Development District
Minneapolis MN	Eliot Park	Not substantially redeveloped
New Orleans LA	Central Business District	Downtown Development District
New Orleans LA	French Quarter	Not substantially redeveloped

talization of Central Cities (NCRCC) based at the University of New Orleans. These case studies were completed in 1992 and 1993 and include basic descriptions of the redevelopment experiences of the four cities in the present study. These case study reports (Lauria et al. 1993; Nelson and Milgroom 1993; Bureau of Governmental Research 1992; Schwartz 1992) have served as the primary data source for our characterizations of the redevelopment experiences of the four cities. They have also served as the primary resource for determining the operative revitalization strategies that guided the actions of private and public redevelopment actors in the four cities we examine.

The areas examined in this chapter correspond as closely as possible either to existing neighborhoods (as they are locally defined), or development/planning districts (as defined by local development and/or planning agencies). The U.S. Census area category designed to correspond to the traditional neighborhood is the census tract (U.S. Bureau of the Census Users Guide 1990, pp. 8–9). Accordingly, census tract data are used as the basis for the description of the social and demographic changes over time (1950–1990) in the neighborhoods of interest in the four cities.

In reality, most neighborhoods are composed of numerous tracts. This fact has required a painstaking process of combining tracts in such a way as to conform to local boundaries. Attendant problems are exacerbated by the fact that frequently both tract numbers and boundaries change over time. These challenges, in turn, are compounded by the additional constraint that locally understood boundaries between neighborhoods (particularly those that have been redeveloped) frequently change as well.

As mentioned, each area examined is composed of several census tracts. In a few cases neighborhoods contain partial tracts. Tract totals, in these cases, are divided as appropriate assuming a proportionate geographic distribution of social and demographic features within these tracts.

While constructing the areas has been methodologically challenging, every effort has been made to balance the need to be true to locally understood boundaries while working with the constraints that tract-level census data impose.

THE DATA: MEASURING IMPROVEMENT AND REVITALIZATION

Social scientists have written a great deal about neighborhood revitalization as it relates to residential integration, but there are no commonly accepted standards by which to judge an area to be "improving" (Goodman and Monti 1996) or "integrated" (Smith 1993). Integration is typically defined in terms of bringing more minorities into areas largely populated by whites. Some scholars speak of integration in terms of retaining white households and attracting new minority households (Taub et al., 1984; Wiese, 1995). Frequently, the presence of comparable numbers of whites and blacks is seen as a sign of integration (Bradburn et al., 1971; Saltman, 1990).

A more flexible standard in assessing the degree to which areas have become integrated has been adopted by some researchers. Thus, integration is present when both blacks and whites are able to maintain a "substantial presence" in a given area. Alternatively, they might share the neighborhood in proportions that reflect their presence in the municipality as a whole (Saltman 1990; Smith 1993).

The present project measures "improvement" in a more complex and detailed way than is typically undertaken in studies of redevelopment and community vitality. Given that many studies of redevelopment argue that economic inequality, population displacement, and gentrification are typically the consequences of community revitalization efforts (Fainstein 1991; Longoria 1994; Lowery 1992; Negry and Zickel 1994; Orr and Stoker 1994; Palen and London 1984; Warren 1994), a more detailed description of community vitality is needed in order to assess whether in fact these are typical impacts of redevelopment, and if so whether they can be associated with particular revitalization strategies and development policies. Further, by measuring community vitality more sensitively one is better able to assess the relative efficacy of a variety of common inner-city revitalization strategies.

The present project conceives of community vitality as not only the presence of a more racially balanced population but also incorporates age and occupational composition, educational attainment, family income, and selected housing characteristics of the community into its definition of "revitalization." Tracking these indicators over an extended time period (1950–1990) allows one to determine whether documented changes in community vitality are reasonably attributable to redevelopment activities or are in fact due to local social and historical patterns of development which long precede the redevelopment activities examined.

Population and Race

Data were collected on the total population, gender, and racial composition of the sixteen neighborhoods. Four racial categories have been selected. They are whites, blacks, Asians, and other. These categories reflect the most consistently reported census categories of the past five decades.

Age Composition

Implicit in the ongoing debate about the concentration of an urban underclass and the decline of inner-city neighborhoods are notions about what is missing from many city neighborhoods (Anderson 1990; Massey et al. 1994; Wilson 1987). Often what is missing from these areas are significant numbers of adults with good jobs.

If the age distribution of a population is skewed toward younger and older, then there are fewer persons who can hold a job and provide for their families, serve as good role models, and assume key leadership positions in the community (Goodman and Monti, 1999). Therefore, a neighborhood that is experiencing revitalization should have a significant number of working-age residents.

Accordingly, a large amount of data were collected that describe the changing age composition in the sixteen neighborhoods. These data allow an effective assessment of the degree to which these neighborhoods (redeveloped and less substantially developed) have managed to retain and/or attract the working population necessary to maintain a viable community.

Numerous age categories are reported by the U.S. census. These categories have changed frequently over the past fifty years. This has required extensive and time-consuming manipulation in order to compare age categories over time accurately. Three age categories are used: 0–19 years old, 20–64 years old, and 65 and over. These categories are designed to measure segments of what can be called the "dependent population" (the very young and old) as well as the "productive" or working-age population.

Occupational Composition

While it is a positive sign if there are more working-age adults in a neighborhood following its redevelopment, it is of limited value if these adults are not employed. Thus, we contend that the number of residents who hold a job is an important consideration in assessing the success of efforts to redevelop central city neighborhoods.

One objective of many central city revitalization efforts has been to expand employment opportunities for area residents by attracting existing businesses to the area, to promote the development of new job-creating small businesses, and/or simply to attract more residents holding jobs. To the extent that redevelopment efforts have fulfilled their promise, there should be more employed residents with better jobs after redevelopment projects are completed than there were prior to the initiation of a revitalization campaign.

Accordingly employment data are tracked for the sixteen neighborhoods of interest, specifically the size of the local labor force as well as the number of employed and unemployed residents.

Presumably the character and quality of jobs held by residents in a redeveloped area will be different from those held by earlier residents and residents of less substantially developed communities. If redevelopment efforts have had their intended effects, we would expect to see residents of redeveloped communities holding better jobs than their predecessors and neighbors. Therefore, data have been collected that allow the tracking of the number of residents working in the following four job sectors over a fifty-year period: managers and professional workers, sales and clerical workers, service employees, and blue-collar workers (operators and laborers).

The census reports numerous job categories and subcategories. As is the case with most census data, these categories frequently change over time. The selected categories reflect the job sectors that have been reported reliably and consistently over time and thus allow for accurate comparisons.

Education

Another indicator of community vitality is the level of education possessed by its residents. This is crucial for both cultural and economic reasons. For redevelopment projects and community revitalization efforts to be successful a population is needed with the skills required to get high-quality jobs and the ability necessary to keep them. It is unlikely that redevelopment and revitalization efforts in themselves "cause" educational attainment to rise; nevertheless, the level of educational attainment possessed by community residents strongly affects its social and economic character and vitality. Accordingly, the numbers of high school and college graduates within each neighborhood were tracked over a fifty-year period. One would expect increasing numbers of highly educated residents in successfully redeveloped neighborhoods.

Income

Another important aspect of the social and economic vitality of a community is the level of income that its residents earn. Needless to say, a higher income gives an individual or family greater control over their lives. This can include expanded choice of where to live, greater opportunities for home ownership, and chances to access the opportunities afforded by good schools.

Thus, income offers an indirect measure of the quality of life of a given community as compared to neighboring communities. Therefore, data on the median family incomes of the neighborhoods of interest over the past five decades were collected. Accordingly, one expects to find rising income levels in successfully redeveloped neighborhoods.

Housing

Finally, data were collected that track the total number of housing units and the number of vacant housing units in each area over the five decades examined. This information allows a description of the changing housing conditions of each neighborhood. One expects to document a higher proportion of occupied housing units in successfully redeveloped areas.

Data Analysis

This chapter examines a series of community case studies of redevelopment projects and their social and economic impacts. Accordingly, its analytical goals reflect the quasi-experimental nature of the project design and the descriptive character of the census data that were analyzed.

The first step in our data analysis has been to examine, in detail, the social and economic changes documented by the census data that took place prior to redevelopment and to compare them to the changes that took place after revitalization efforts were undertaken.

Then the social and economic experiences of the redeveloped areas were systematically compared with those of adjacent communities which remain relatively free of substantial redevelopment projects. The results of these comparisons are described in the pages to follow.

THE CASE OF ATLANTA

Underground Atlanta—A Supportively Developed Project

Underground Atlanta is a festival marketplace developed during the 1980s and located in the south-central end of downtown Atlanta. This project, while utilizing considerable amounts of public financing, can be fairly characterized as being "supportively" developed. The role of the public sector was primarily to facilitate the development of this project by leveraging financing, making infrastructure improvements, and committing future tax revenues to the redevelopment area:

The cost of Underground Atlanta was a little over $141 million. Over $112 million of this was funded publicly. As early as 1984, an Urban Development Action Grant of $10 million was awarded to the city for the Underground project. The most significant public funding source, however, was an $85 million bond issued by the Downtown Development Authority (DDA) for the development of Underground and its necessary infrastructure. The DDA was given authority to issue this money through revenue bonds without needing public consent or a specific referendum. Twenty one million dollars in sales tax revenues and CDBG funds were also issued for the project by the city. Subsequently, $6 million came from the Fulton County Building Authority for the development of parking facilities. (Nelson and Milgroom 1993, p. 28)

Our analysis of the social and economic consequences of this revitalization effort focused on two neighborhoods: Summerhill and Atlanta University. Following several telephone interviews with local observers and officials of the Atlanta City Planning Department, it was determined that these neighborhoods were quite similar in terms of social, demographic, and economic composition prior to the development of the Underground.

We were told that Summerhill was one of several local neighborhoods likely affected by the Underground project. We also learned that the Atlanta University neighborhood had not been noticeably affected.

We tracked social and demographic changes in the Summerhill and Atlanta University neighborhoods from 1950–1990. A detailed statistical profile of each neighborhood examined was prepared as part of the research conducted for this chapter. In the interest of brevity these data were not included with this volume. Interested parties should contact the authors if they wish to obtain a copy of the full statistical appendix to this chapter.

It is clear that the Summerhill neighborhood experienced substantial social and demographic changes we would associate with increasing community vitality. Notably, its residents became more vital in terms of their age distribution, educational attainment, and occupational composition.

In contrast, the Atlanta University neighborhood experienced declines in its working-age population while its residents became less well-educated and experienced substantial increases in their rate of unemployment.

The occupational composition of both neighborhoods changed similarly. Both Summerhill and Atlanta University witnessed a decline in tra-

Table 2–2
Social and Demographic Changes since the Underground Redevelopment Project

Characteristic	Affected Area *Summerhill*	Adjacent Area *Atlanta University*
Population	Stable	Stable
Racial composition	Mixed	Segregated
Age composition	Growing 20–64	Shrinking 20–64
Educational attainment	Increase in well-educated	Decline in well-educated
Family income	Substantial increases	Relatively smaller increases
Unemployment	Stable	Increasing
Occupational composition	Highly skilled	Highly skilled
Housing occupancy	High vacancy	High vacancy

Source: Goodman and Monti, 1996

ditional blue-collar jobs while an increasing, although relatively small, proportion of their populations occupied professional and managerial occupations.

The World Congress Center—An Actively Developed Project

The World Congress Center is a major convention center that opened in 1976. Substantial development followed most notably the construction of the Georgia Dome, a major multiuse stadium complex. These projects can be fairly characterized as involving the use of an "active" redevelopment strategy. The role of the public sector has been critical to these projects, involving very large amounts of public funds, the commitment of future tax revenues, and a substantial involvement in project siting and planning:

> The World Congress Center was constructed in three distinct phases, each receiving extensive city or state input. The initial two phases were funded through State General Obligation Bonds. The first development began in 1975 with a cost of $35 million. The second development

began in 1985 at a cost of $103 million. Both actions required specific State General Assembly approval in order to allocate sufficient funds. In essence, most of these bonds were floated through state-sponsored programs. Recently, the state approved another expansion expected to cost $75 million. (Nelson and Milgroom, 1993, p. 47)

The $200 million cost of the Georgia Dome project was financed through city issued revenue bonds. Revenue generated by the facility and a portion of Atlanta's city transit and occupancy tax receipts have been used to make the revenue bond payments (Nelson and Milgroom 1993).

Both the Vine City and the English Avenue neighborhoods are located adjacent to the World Congress Center facility. It is clear that neither neighborhood experienced anything resembling revitalization. The persistence of racial segregation and significant increases in the unemployment rate in both of these communities stand in stark contrast to the apparently successful economic impact these facilities have had on the larger city as a whole (Nelson and Milgroom 1993). See Table 2–3 for a summary of the social and demographic changes experienced by each neighborhood.

Table 2–3
Social and Demographic Changes since the World Congress Center Redevelopment

Characteristic	Affected Area *Vine City*	Adjacent Area *English Avenue*
Population	Decreasing	Decreasing
Racial composition	Segregated	Segregated
Age composition	Stable	Stable
Educational attainment	More high school graduates	More high school graduates
Family income	Steady increase	Steady increase
Unemployment	Substantial increase	Substantial increase
Occupational composition	Declining job base	Declining job base
Housing occupancy	High vacancy	High vacancy

Source: Goodman and Monti, 1996

THE CASE OF MINNEAPOLIS

The Loring Park Development District— A Supportively Developed Project

The Loring Park Development District is located in a neighborhood of the same name just south of the downtown area in Minneapolis. Its use as a tax increment district designed to promote redevelopment began in 1972. Since this date the city has directed $37 million of its local tax revenues to this area. These funds have been used to promote and encourage private development efforts (Schwartz 1992). Therefore, we have characterized this revitalization effort as involving a supportive revitalization strategy:

> The Loring Development District involved several major projects, some of which were not completed until the early 1980s. These included several large housing developments, with about one-fourth of the total units reserved for low and moderate income residents, a Hyatt Regency hotel and merchandise mart, Orchestra Hall, and campuses for two educational institutions. In addition, the Loring Park Development District financed the four-block extension of the Nicollet Mall towards Loring Park. It also paid for the Loring Greenway, a pedestrian walkway that links the Nicollet Mall directly to Loring Park and beyond to the city's well known Guthrie Theater and Walker Art Institute. (Ibid. p. 21).

Our analysis of the social and economic consequences of this revitalization effort focused on two neighborhoods, Loring and Eliot Park. Following several telephone interviews with local observers and officials of the Minneapolis City Planning Department, it was determined that these neighborhoods were quite similar in terms of their social, demographic, and economic composition prior to the presence of the Loring Park Development District.

Both the Loring and Eliot Park neighborhoods experienced changes we would associate with revitalization following this supportive development experience. These neighborhoods appear to have attracted more racially mixed and better educated residents.

The Hennepin County Government Center— An Actively Developed Project

The Hennepin County Government Center is a public facility that is home to a variety of municipal offices serving Hennepin County, Minnesota. It was planned and funded publicly and therefore we characterize it as an actively developed redevelopment project:

> The Hennepin County Government Center houses courts and administrative offices for Hennepin County in two 550,000 square foot towers connected by a glass atrium. The twin towers were completed in 1973 at a cost of $41.8 million. Besides its prominence in the downtown skyline, the Government Center is significant for its location several blocks east of Nicollet Mall. It was one of the first office buildings to be built in the area of downtown designated in the city's original downtown plan for office development. (Schwartz 1992, p. 22).

Our analysis of the social and economic consequences of this revitalization effort focused on two neighborhoods, Downtown West and Downtown East. Following several telephone interviews with local observers and officials of the Minneapolis City Planning Department, it was determined that these neighborhoods were quite similar in terms of social, demographic, and economic composition prior to the presence of the Hennepin County Government Center.

The Government Center is located in the Downtown West neighborhood. We determined that the most comparable neighborhood was the

Table 2–4
Social and Demographic Changes since the
Revitalization of Loring Park

Characteristic	Affected Area *Loring Park*	Adjacent Area *Eliot Park*
Population	Stable and growing	Stable and declining
Racial composition	Becoming mixed	More mixed
Age composition	Growing 20–64	Growing 20–64
Educational attainment	More well-educated	More well-educated
Family income	Substantial increase	Slight increase
Unemployment	Slight increase	Slight increase
Occupational composition	White-collar increasing	White-collar increasing
Housing occupancy	Stable	Increasing

Source: Goodman and Monti, 1996

Downtown East neighborhood. However, it was not entirely clear, to us or to local observers, whether the east side of the downtown area was affected by this development project. Rather than choose a better "control" site that was less socially comparable, we opted for the more accurate comparison recognizing the real possibility that the impacts of this project spilled over into the Downtown East neighborhood.

We tracked social and demographic changes in the Downtown West and East neighborhoods from 1950–1990. A summary of these results is presented below (See Table 2–5).

It appears that both of Minneapolis's downtown neighborhoods experienced changes consistent with our definitions of "revitalization" following the development of the Hennepin County Government Center. Additionally, significant office and retail development occurred in these areas following this experience (Schwartz 1992).

THE CASE OF PORTLAND

Oregon Convention Center—A Supportively Developed Project

The Oregon Convention Center Urban Renewal District is located on the east side of downtown Portland. It was developed by the Portland Bureau of Planning during the 1980s. The revitalization strategy for this area has involved facilitating and providing incentives for privately supported economic development activities. The primary device used to promoting private sector involvement in this development area has been tax increment financing (TIF). The first major project in this development area was the Oregon Convention Center. The Convention Center project was funded by both public and private funds (Nelson and Milgroom 1993). Thus, we characterize the role of the public sector in this area as largely supportive:

> The plan calls for adopting detailed urban design guidelines to help preserve the unique nature of the district. It also establishes priorities for economic development and methods for stimulating private sector involvement . . . the anchor development within this district is the Oregon Convention Center. This 17 acre facility was built in 1990. It is sandwiched between the Memorial Coliseum and Interstate–5. A MAX (Metropolitan Area Express) station provides additional transportation options to employees and visitors. Its total project cost was $85 million of which $65 million were [sic] raised from the sale of a general obligation bond and $15 million was paid by the State of Ore-

Table 2–5
Social and Demographic Changes since the Development of Hennepin County

Characteristic	Affected Area *Downtown West*	Adjacent Area *Downtown East*
Population	Becoming stable	Increasing
Racial composition	Becoming mixed	Becoming mixed
Age composition	Remaining stable	Remaining stable
Educational attainment	Increasing	Increasing
Family income	Substantial increase	Substantial increase
Unemployment	Increasing	Slight decrease
Occupational composition	White-collar increasing	White-collar increasing
Housing occupancy	Increasing	Increasing

Source: Goodman and Monti, 1996

gon. The remaining sum was paid by a local improvement district that includes most of the businesses that will benefit from the convention center (Nelson and Milgroom 1993, p.72).

Our analysis of the social and economic consequences of this revitalization effort focused on two neighborhoods: the Lloyd District and Goose Hollow. Following several telephone interviews with local observers and demographers at the Portland Bureau of Planning, it was determined that these neighborhoods were quite similar in terms of social, demographic, and economic composition prior to the implementation of the development plan.

The Lloyd District neighborhood was the area in which these developments took place. We also determined that the Goose Hollow neighborhood had not been noticeably affected.

We tracked social and demographic changes in the Lloyd District and Goose Hollow neighborhoods from 1950–1990. A summary of these results is presented in Table 2–6.

The changes evident in the Lloyd District and the Goose Hollow neighborhoods suggest that they have both experienced some degree of revitalization following the implementation of the development plan described above.

Table 2–6
Social and Demographic Changes since the
Convention Center Redevelopment

Characteristic	Affected Area *Lloyd District*	Adjacent Area *Goose Hollow*
Population	Stable	Stable
Racial composition	Slightly more mixed	Slightly more mixed
Age composition	Growing 20–64	Growing 20–64
Educational attainment	Slight decrease	Slight decrease
Family income	Substantial increase	Substantial increase
Unemployment	Stable	Stable
Occupational composition	White-collar increasing	White-collar increasing
Housing occupancy	Stable	Stable

Source: Goodman and Monti, 1996

The Portland Transit Mall and MAX—
An Actively Developed Project

The Portland Transit Mall and MAX (Metropolitan Area Express) were planned and developed in an effort to provide an effective mass transportation system which served the needs of downtown Portland and the larger metropolitan area. The Transit Mall restricts automobile access and substantially enhances pedestrian access to the downtown area. MAX, a light rail transit system, is part of a larger regional development effort designed to "balance the area's transportation system, reduce traffic congestion, help to contain growth, and foster dense and more favorable development" (Nelson and Milgroom 1993, p. 57). These projects were entirely planned and funded by public agencies. Consequently, we characterize their revitalization strategies as active:

> The Transit Mall and MAX were financed primarily through federal assistance under the Urban Mass Transportation Act (UMTA) of 1965. Eighty percent of the $15 million Transit Mall was funded from the UMTA with the balance funded by Tri-Met (Tri-County Metropolitan Transportation District of Oregon). UMTA and other federal agencies absorbed 83 percent of MAX's total $214 million cost, which included

the reconstruction of one segment of I–84 in the Portland area. Much of the federal money had been earmarked for a new freeway through Portland's southeast neighborhood, but when the city became successful in having state and federal highway agencies cancel the freeway, the money remained available to finance the light-rail development. (Nelson and Milgroom 1993, p. 58)

Our analysis of the social and economic consequences of this revitalization effort focused on two neighborhoods, the Central Business District and Central East-Side. Following several telephone interviews with local observers and demographers at the Portland Bureau of Planning, it was determined that these neighborhoods were quite similar in terms of social, demographic, and economic composition prior to the implementation of these revitalization efforts.

The Central Business District was the area in which these developments took place. We also determined through telephone interviews with City Planning officials that the Central East-Side neighborhood had not been noticeably affected by these projects.

We tracked social and demographic changes in the Central Business District and Central East-Side neighborhoods from 1950–1990. A summary of these results is presented in Table 2–7.

The changes experienced in the Central Business District and Central East-Side neighborhoods suggest that they have both experienced some degree of revitalization following the implementation of the revitalization plan described above.

THE CASE OF NEW ORLEANS

The Downtown Development District— A Supportive Revitalization Effort

The Downtown Development District (DDD) (formerly the Core Area Development District) is a special taxing district created by state law in 1977. The purpose of the district is to upgrade the central business area of the city by providing additional services, such as police, sanitation, and cultural events and to provide capital improvements such as sidewalks, streets, and pedestrian malls. The services and capital improvements provided by DDD taxes are in addition to those otherwise provided by the city. The DDD has a yearly budget of approximately $4 million (Bureau of Governmental Research 1992, pp. 20–21).

Table 2–7
Social and Demographic Changes since the Transit Mall/
MAX Redevelopment

Characteristic	Affected Area *Central Business District*	Adjacent Area *Central East-Side*
Population	Stable	Stable
Racial composition	Slightly more mixed	Slightly more mixed
Age composition	Stable	Stable
Educational attainment	More college graduates	More college graduates
Family income	Substantial increase	Substantial increase
Unemployment	Stable	Declining
Occupational composition	White-collar increasing	White-collar increasing
Housing occupancy	Stable	Stable

Source: Goodman and Monti, 1996

We characterize the Downtown Development District as a support-ive revitalization effort due to its emphasis on encouraging private devel-opment through local improvement campaigns. Our analysis of the social and economic consequences of this revitalization effort focused on two neighborhoods, the Central Business District (CBD) and the French Quarter. The DDD's efforts are concentrated on the Central Business District; therefore, it was selected as our affected area. Following tele-phone interviews with a variety of local observers and officials from the City Planning Department, we selected the French Quarter as our com-parison neighborhood.

According to staff members at both the DDD and the Planning Depart-ment, the French Quarter's restrictions on development for the purposes of historical preservation and its similar social and demographic composi-tion prior to revitalization efforts make it a suitable comparison site. How-ever, the overall downtown area of New Orleans has seen a substantial amount of development in recent years. As a result, conclusions about the impacts of specific redevelopment projects need to be made with some care.

We tracked social and demographic changes in the Central Business District and the French Quarter from 1950–1990. A summary of these re-sults is presented in Table 2–8.

The changes experienced in the Central Business District and the French Quarter suggest that both areas experienced some degree of revitalization following the implementation of the revitalization plan described above. However, it appears that the Central Business District experienced a greater degree of revitalization, as reflected in its more racially mixed and occupationally white-collar residential composition in the years following the appearance of the Downtown Development District. There is some reason to believe that the revitalization experienced in this area of downtown New Orleans may be in some part due to other redevelopment efforts in the CBD, efforts that began in preparation for the World's Fair in 1984 (Bureau of Governmental Research 1992). Consequently, conclusions associating particular revitalization strategies and community outcomes must be made cautiously.

The Louisiana Superdome—An Actively Developed Project

The Superdome was completed in August, 1976 at an approximate cost of $163 million. The Dome was financed through the issuance of bonds by the Louisiana Stadium and Exposition District, a political subdivision of the state. The bonds were secured by a hotel-motel

Table 2–8
Social and Demographic Changes since Revitalization of the Downtown Development District

Characteristic	Affected Area *CBD*	Adjacent Area *French Quarter*
Population	Declining	Declining
Racial composition	Integrated	Segregated
Age composition	Growing 20–64 group	Stable
Educational attainment	Substantial increase	High school grad. inc./ college decrease
Family income	Substantial increase	Substantial increase
Unemployment	Substantial increase	Substantial increase
Occupational composition	White-collar increasing	White-collar increasing
Housing occupancy	Increase in vacant units	Increase in vacant units

Source: Goodman and Monti, 1996

occupancy tax levied by the stadium district in Orleans and Jefferson Parishes.

The City had no direct responsibility for the cost of the Superdome nor its operating expenses. The Superdome is owned by the Louisiana Stadium and Exposition District, which leases the Superdome to the State of Louisiana. In July, 1977 the state entered into a contract with HMC Management Corporation, a private subsidiary of the Hyatt Corporation, for the operation of the Superdome. (Bureau of Governmental Research 1992, pp. 19–20)

We characterize the Superdome as an actively developed project due to its almost exclusive reliance on the public sector for its funding and planning.

Our analysis of the social and economic consequences of this revitalization effort focused on two areas: Central City North and Central City South. These two areas are actually part of a larger Central City neighborhood. They were selected following telephone interviews with local observers and staff members at the City Planning Department.

The area we refer to as "Central City North" is composed of a number of census tracts that are immediately adjacent to the Superdome site. Central City South is a collection of census tracts separated from the Superdome site by the Central City North area. We designated Central City North as the affected neighborhood due to its immediate proximity to the Superdome site and Central City South as the adjacent neighborhood due to its relative distance from the project area.

We tracked social and demographic changes in Central City North and South from 1950–1990. A summary of these results is presented in Table 2–9.

It is clear that neither portion of the Central City neighborhood experienced anything resembling revitalization following the development of the Superdome. The persistence of racial segregation and significant increases in the unemployment rate in both of these areas stand in stark contrast to the apparently successful economic impact the Superdome has had on the larger city as a whole.

Of the eight case studies conducted in the four selected cities, five of the case studies appear to display what may be termed a "spill over" effect, with development taking place beyond the targeted areas of the development projects. It is also possible, though, that other local factors may be at work. In Minneapolis, the Eliot Park neighborhood experienced revitalization similar to the targeted area of the Loring Development District, and Downtown East experienced development similar to

Table 2–9
Social and Demographic Changes since the
Louisiana Superdome Project

Characteristic	Affected Area *Central City North*	Adjacent Area *Central City South*
Population	Declining	Declining
Racial composition	Slight increase in mix	Stable
Age composition	Stable	Stable
Educational attainment	Stable	Stable
Family income	Modest increase	Modest increase
Unemployment	Substantial increase	Substantial increase
Occupational composition	White-collar increasing	White-collar increasing
Housing occupancy	Increase in vacant units	Increase in vacant units

Source: Goodman and Monti, 1996

the targeted area of Downtown West. In Portland, Oregon, the Goose Hollow neighborhood experienced revitalization similar to the targeted neighborhood of the Lloyd District, and the Central-East Side experienced revitalization similar to that experienced by targeted Central Business District. In New Orleans, the French Quarter, as well as the targeted Central Business District, experienced revitalization. In each of these cases, further in-depth on-site investigation will be required to determine the specific factors responsible for the observed revitalization.

DISCUSSION

The social and economic impact of both the four actively and four supportively developed projects we examined was generally positive (see Table 2–10).

However, there appears to be some evidence that suggests strongly that these approaches have substantially different impacts under particular circumstances. One important lesson is that there is a crucial distinction to be drawn between the economic development of the city as a whole and the social and economic revitalization of central city neighborhoods.

The experiences of the Atlanta and New Orleans neighborhoods affected by the active development of large multiuse stadium complexes suggests that while these efforts appear to have had a strong positive im-

Table 2–10

Central City	Development	Project Description	Strategy	Effect on Neighborhood
Atlanta	World Congress Center	Convention Center	Active	No positive impact
Atlanta	Underground	Festival marketplace	Supportive	Revitalized
Minneapolis	Loring Park Development District	Tax district	Supportive	Revitalized
Minneapolis	Hennepin County Govt. Center	Government building	Active	Revitalized
Portland	Transit Mall/MAX	Transit upgrade	Active	Revitalized
Portland	Convention center	Tax district	Supportive	Revitalized
New Orleans	Superdome	Athletic stadium	Active	No positive impact
New Orleans	Downtown Development District	Tax district	Supportive	Revitalized

pact on the economic vitality of the city as a whole, they contribute little to the social and community vitality of the neighborhoods in which they are developed.

In contrast, all Atlanta and New Orleans neighborhoods affected by supportive development efforts experienced social and demographic changes we would associate with improving community vitality, including attracting a more racially mixed population.

It is important to consider whether the changes we document and characterize as "improving" are simply evidence of a process of gentrification in these areas. When we closely examine the experiences of the neighborhoods we contend show "improvement" or increasing community vitality, this does not appear to be the case. In a gentrifying neighborhood we would expect to see the displacement of existing lower-class black residents and their replacement by new more upscale white residents.

What we have documented in the supportively developed neighborhoods in Atlanta and New Orleans is a different pattern. Prior to redevelopment these areas were losing considerable numbers of white residents and gaining considerable numbers of black residents. The impact of supportive revitalization efforts does not appear to have reversed this trend; rather, it appears to have stopped "white flight" and contributed to a more stable racial composition in these communities.

In Minneapolis and Portland the implementation of both supportive and active redevelopment strategies preceded community revitalization. The relatively smaller size of their downtown areas (as compared to Atlanta and New Orleans) makes it more difficult to associate the "improvement" we document with a particular revitalization strategy. Furthermore, this makes it more problematic to contend that the impacts of these strategies are contained in specific neighborhoods within their downtown areas than it is in Atlanta and New Orleans, where the areas are larger and the differences more apparent.

Additionally, the social and economic problems facing both Minneapolis and Portland, as reflected in the residential composition of their downtown neighborhoods, are considerably less severe than those faced by Atlanta and New Orleans. This is not to diminish the accomplishments of redevelopment efforts in Minneapolis and Portland as much as to recognize the different scale of the problems they faced and addressed in planning and funding their respective development activities.

FUTURE RESEARCH DIRECTIONS

It is clear that if the impact of public redevelopment strategies on central city communities is to be fully understood, each city will require a site visit. This will allow the confirmation of whether our descriptions of increasing or decreasing community vitality in a given neighborhood are consistent with the views and experiences of its community residents. Consequently, these visits should involve a number of in-depth interviews with community residents.

Additionally, a variety of private developers and public development officials should be interviewed. This will allow a much more comprehensive understanding of what actually motivated public and private redevelopment efforts in these cities as well as allowing a more sensitive assessment of community vitality.

The most critical information required for informed policy decisions on how we can revitalize our central cities in an era of shrinking federal funds is a clear understanding of which strategies do and do not work. Given the scope of the problems facing American central cities and a contemporary political reality that is likely to increase the dependence of public redevelopment actors on their private sector counterparts, it is clear that a more complete understanding of the social impacts of central city redevelopment and a more detailed description of the impacts of publicly and privately sponsored redevelopment activities is needed now more than ever.

REFERENCES

Anderson, Elijah. 1990. *Street wise.* Chicago: The University of Chicago Press)

Beauregard, Robert. 1985. Politics, ideology, and theories of gentrification. *Journal of Urban Affairs,* 7(4): 51–62.

Bell, Daniel. 1973. *The coming of postindustrial society.* New York: Basic Books.

Bradburn, Norman, Seymour Sudman, and Galen Gockel. 1971. *Side by side: integrated neighborhoods in America.* Chicago: Quadrangle Books.

Bright, Elise, Richard Cole, Patricia Matthews, and Sherman Wyman. 1993. Central city revitalization: The Fort Worth experience. Working Paper No. 9. New Orleans: College of Urban and Public Affairs UNO.

Bureau of Governmental Research. 1992. Inventory of economic development programs in the city of New Orleans, 1970–1992. Working Paper No. 2. New Orleans: College of Urban and Public Affairs UNO.

Cicin-Sain, Biliana. 1980. The costs and benefits of neighborhood revitalization. In Donald Rosenthal (ed.) *Urban Revitalization, Urban Affairs Annual Series, Volume 18,* Beverly Hills, CA: Sage Publications.

Fainstein, Susan. 1991. Rejoinder to: Questions of abstraction in studies in the new urban politics. *Journal of Urban Affairs, 13*(3): 281–288.

Goodman, Michael, and Daniel Monti. 1999. Corporately sponsored redevelopment campaigns and the social stability of urban neighborhoods. *Journal of Urban Affairs, 21*(1): 101–127.

Goodman, Michael, and Daniel Monti. 1996. Appendix to social, economic, and demographic characteristics of sixteen central city neighborhoods. (Unpublished Report.)

Lauria, Mickey, Robert Whelan, and Alma Young. 1993. Urban revitalization strategies and plans in New Orleans, 1970–1993. Working Paper No. 10. New Orleans: College of Urban and Public Affairs UNO.

Longoria, Thomas. 1994. Empirical analysis of the city limits typology. *Urban Affairs Quarterly, 30*(1): 102–113.

Lowery, David, Ruth Hoogland DeHoog, and William Lyons. 1992. Citizenship in the empowered locality: An elaboration, a critique, and a partial test. *Urban Affairs Quarterly, 28*(1): 69–103.

Massey, Douglas and Nancy Denton. 1993. American apartheid: Segregation and the making of the underclass. Cambridge: Harvard University Press.

Massey, Douglas, Andrew Gross, and Kumiko Shibuya. 1994. Migration, segregation, and the concentration of poverty. *American Sociological Review, 59*(3): 425–445.

Monti, Daniel. 1990. *Race, redevelopment, and the new company town.* Albany: State University of New York Press.

Mumphrey, Anthony and Karen A. Pinell. 1992. New Orleans and the top 25 cities: Central city and metropolitan dualities. Working Paper No. 1. New Orleans: College of Urban and Public Affairs UNO.

Negrey, Cynthia and Mary Beth Zickel. 1994. Industrial shifts and uneven development: Patterns of growth and decline in U.S. metropolitan areas. *Urban Affairs Quarterly, 30*(1): 27–47.

Nelson, Arthur and Jeffrey Milgroom. 1993. The role of regional development management in central city revitalization: case studies and comparisons of development patterns in Atlanta, Georgia and Portland, Oregon. Working Paper No. 6. New Orleans: College of Urban and Public Affairs UNO.

Orr, Marion and Gerry Stoker. 1994. Urban regimes and leadership in Detroit. *Urban Affairs Quarterly, 30*(1): 48–73.

Palen, John and Bruce London, eds. 1984. *Gentrification, displacement, and neighborhood revitalization.* Albany: State University of New York Press.

Palen, John and Chava Nachmias. 1984. Revitalization in a working-class neighborhood. In *Gentrification, displacement, and neighborhood revitalization,* Palen, John and Bruce London (eds.). Albany: State University of New York Press.

Reich, Robert. 1992. *The work of nations.* New York: Vintage.

Rogowsky, Edward and Ronald Berkman. 1993. New York City's 'outer-borough' development strategy: Case studies in urban revitalization. Working Paper No. 8. New Orleans: College of Urban and Public Affairs UNO.

Saltman, Juliet. 1990. *A Fragile Movement: The Struggle for Neighborhood Stabilization.* New York: Greenwood Press.

Schwartz, Alex. 1992. Rebuilding downtown: A case study of Minneapolis. Working paper No. 3. New Orleans: College of Urban and Public Affairs UNO.

Smith, Richard. 1993. Creating stable racially integrated communities: A review. *Journal of Urban Affairs, 15*(2): 115–141.

Squires, Gregory. 1994. *Capital and communities in black and white.* Albany: State University of New York Press.

Stone, Clarence, Marion Orr, Timothy Ross, and David Imbroscio. 1993. Baltimore and the human-investment challenge. Working paper No. 5. New Orleans: College of Urban and Public Affairs UNO.

Taub, Richard, D. Taylor, and Jan Dunham. 1984. *Paths of neighborhood change.* Chicago: University of Chicago Press.

U.S. Bureau of the Census Users guide. Washington, DC: Government Printing Office.

U.S. Bureau of the Census. Census of population and housing, 1950–1990 (STF3A). Washington, DC: Government Printing Office.

Warren, Stacey. 1994. Disneyfication of the metropolis: Popular resistance in Seattle. *Journal of Urban Affairs, 16*(2): 89–108.

Whelan, Robert, Alma Young, and Mickey Lauria. 1993. Urban regimes and racial politics: New Orleans during the Barthelemy years. Working Paper No. 7. New Orleans: College of Urban and Public Affairs UNO.

Wiese, Andrew. 1995. "Neighborhood diversity: Social change, ambiguity, and fair housing since 1968. *Journal of Urban Affairs, 17*(2): 107–130.

Wilson, William Julius. 1987. *The truly disadvantaged: The inner city, the underclass, and public policy.* Chicago: The University of Chicago Press.

CHAPTER 3

TOADS: Instruments of Urban Revitalization

ELISE BRIGHT

The neighborhood is the setting in which people make their largest financial investments, spend most of their free time, and raise their children. Its importance is difficult to overemphasize: "Next to what goes on in your mind and what goes on in your home, probably the most important thing in your world is what goes on in your neighborhood" (Community Action Program 1967). Clearly, if the government is to fulfill its legal mandate of protecting public health, safety, and welfare, it must do what it can to ensure that our neighborhoods are safe, sanitary, and provide a high quality of life. Yet many inner-city neighborhoods are obviously far from ideal; residents live with serious threats to their health, safety, and welfare every day in many parts of urban America, and a high quality of life is an unfulfilled dream. This chapter is organized into four major sections: introduction, methodology, project summaries, and recommendations.

Background

Greenberg and Popper (1994) described one major difficulty faced by inner-city neighborhoods: the proliferation of TOADS (temporarily obsolete, abandoned, derelict sites). This research stemmed from a growing awareness on the part of the author that TOADS in many low-income inner-city residential neighborhoods are actually owned by various levels of government. This property ends in government hands for a variety of reasons; two of the more common reasons include failure of owners to pay their local property taxes (thus resulting in city or county ownership), and acquisition for use in urban renewal or highway projects that

45

were never completed (the state or federal government may retain ownership in some of these cases, although transfer of ownership to the city can occur if a redevelopment project is proposed).

In less poverty-stricken areas of town, loan foreclosure by the U.S. Department of Housing and Urban Development (HUD) or the Veterans' Administration (VA), along with property acquired by the now-defunct Resolution Trust Corporation (RTC) as a result of bank failure, also become important pathways for government ownership. Military base closings, school closings, unused roadways, and abandoned railroad rights of way also provide surplus land in some cities.

Initial research revealed that in the vast majority of cases these properties are active contributors to neighborhood decline. Governments are often unaware of their ownership of these properties; Greenberg and Popper (1994) concluded, "most cities lacked comprehensive data on the numbers and types of abandoned sites within their jurisdiction. Sometimes, cities had good figures on one type of abandoned property—housing, for instance—but could only guess when asked about numbers of abandoned commercial and industrial structures. Some cities kept accurate records on vacant lots but were less certain about the numbers of properties with standing abandoned buildings" (p. 18).

Thus, it is not surprising that such properties often continued to be ignored and neglected even after government acquisition. They became physically dilapidated; many were abandoned or became unofficial homeless shelters, and some were even used as havens for those engaging in illegal activities. As Marino, Rosser and Rozran (1979) explain, "There is often a considerable quantity of tax delinquent property in deteriorated neighborhoods. Investigation of the relationship between housing abandonment and tax delinquency has indicated that there is a positive correlation between multifamily property which is tax delinquent for two or more years and property abandonment (within five years) . . . abandonment rapidly reduces the marketability of a neighborhood and restricts residents' access to conventional credit." Greenberg and Popper (1994) make the point more strongly: "Abandoned properties produce no legal revenues. They lower nearby property values, create public costs, and are expensive to police. They often frighten residents and business owners into leaving the vicinity, producing more abandonment . . . they also mean a substantial loss to the municipality in foregone taxes" (p. 11).

Research Goals

Drawing on studies of successful downtown revitalization, the author hypothesized that ownership of TOADS by the government could present an invaluable opportunity to improve low-income central city neighborhoods. As Greenberg and Popper (1994) point out, "TOADS often lie on potentially valuable inner-city land" (p. 24). Therefore, the author set out to determine whether, in fact, these properties had ever been used successfully to catalyze inner-city residential neighborhood revitalization. More specifically, the goal was to determine how cities have utilized government-owned properties successfully to revitalize low-income neighborhoods.

Although successful efforts did focus on reuse of TOADS, success could not be achieved through property reuse alone; many other urban ills also had to be addressed. Thus, the research efforts also document related activities that appeared important in low-income neighborhood revitalization.

Definitional Issues

Before beginning the research, two methodological difficulties had to be resolved. First, the term "revitalization" had to be defined; second, it had to be determined what constitutes "success." Based on an extensive literature review, "revitalization" is defined by the author as "changes that improve neighborhood residents' quality of life." There are some very important parts of this definition that merit further discussion.

Quality of Life: Many scholars have attempted to define and develop measures of quality of life (Cole, Smith, and Taebel 1984; Gould 1986). Likewise, many scholars have identified a wide range of problems—that is, barriers to a high quality of life—faced by residents of very low-income inner-city areas (Feagin and Parker 1990; Squires 1994; Anderson, Hadawi, and Shuroro 1995).

After a thorough review of this work, the author developed a typology of indicators to measure quality of life in inner-city residential areas; these fall into four broad categories: neighborhood safety, services, shelter, and social support. Table 3–1 summarizes the principal indicators that constitute each category—the list is by no means comprehensive. Issues of measurement and quantification are discussed in the section on methodology.

Success: "Success" in neighborhood revitalization, generally, is defined as improvement in quality of life indicators (listed in Table 3–1).

The most successful projects are those with significant improvement in all of them. In reality, however, this is rarely the case; rather, one finds either a project that has resulted in a great deal of improvement in a small number of indicators (that is, its results are characterized by depth), or a project that has slightly improved many (that is, its results are characterized by breadth). Likewise, the issue of "success for whom?" becomes important. Should a project that achieves improvement in the indicators by replacing existing residents with more affluent ones be considered successful? These issues are discussed in the following section.

METHODOLOGY

Quantitative or Qualitative Approach?

Each item in Table 3–1 should ideally be studied in order to obtain a measure of the quality of life in a given neighborhood; in reality, however, data availability constraints make quantification difficult. There are several problems—for example, the timing of data collection with respect to the beginning and completion dates of revitalization projects; the area in which data collection occurred being incompatible with the project impact area; invalid data collection and/or analysis methods being used; the ability to compare data collected in one city with another or in one neighborhood with others; obtaining data on different indicators for the same geographic area; and determining what proportion of positive change in a neighborhood indicator is explained by the revitalization project, as opposed to outside factors. Additionally, quantitative data is simply not available for some of the most important indicators—for example, the amount of money flowing into a neighborhood from crack cocaine dealing before and after a revitalization project, or information on the number of addicts. Thus, one is faced with either focusing only on those aspects that are readily quantifiable, or relying on local experts to review the entire list of indicators and direct the researcher to those neighborhoods that ranked poorly on most indicators and have subsequently improved.

Realizing that in every city local residents can identify the "worst" parts of town despite a lack of quantitative data on many quality of life indicators, and that those involved in neighborhood development are well-versed in identifying instances of neighborhood improvement by synthesizing a vast storehouse of personal knowledge, the author relied on interviews with local experts.

Table 3–1
Quality of Life Indicators

Safety

- Rates of violent crime and crimes against property (arson, burglary, etc.)
- Rates of death, particularly for persons under 65 (infant mortality, miscarriage, cancer, suicide, etc.)
- Rates of alcohol, nicotine, other drug addiction, and drug dealing
- Degree of exposure to environmental toxins (lead-based paint, brownfields, air pollution, etc.)
- Access to medical care, fire and police assistance

Services

- Level of government services (water, sewer, street repair, garbage service, sidewalks, landscaping, parks, etc.)
- Access to business services (employment opportunities, shopping, entertainment, offices, etc.) even for those without private cars
- Level of social services (primary, secondary, trade, and college education; child care; shelters and emergency intervention and placement; delivery of food and medicine; etc.)

Shelter

- Presence of affordable housing in good condition, appropriately designed (for extended families, disabled residents, the homeless, elderly individuals, and other types of nonnuclear households)
- Access to home ownership
- Level of neighborhood maintenance (code enforcement, litter control, vacant/abandoned property maintenance, etc.)

Social Support

- Access to an informal network of people (relatives, friends, neighbors, interest groups) of varying incomes, ages, etc.
- Urban design that provides opportunities for meeting, and being with, a variety of people while discouraging crime (defensible space, neotraditional design, urban villages)
- Access to local political power

Success: Depth or Breadth?

An extensive review of definitions including quality of life, successful downtown revitalization factors (Frieden and Sagalyn 1992; Gratz 1994, Wagner, Joder, and Mumphrey 1995), failed efforts (Mier 1993; Medoff and Sklar 1994; Rooney 1995), the causes of inner-city problems (Byrum 1992; Pratt Institute 1992; Gratz 1994), and the author's own work in inner-city areas, has led to a novel synthesis. The inner-city is characterized by an extremely complex, interlocking web of social, economic, and physical activities and entities which functions very much like an ecological web; perhaps one could refer to it as a "civicological web." In particular, the existence of this web means that an action that affects one aspect or strand—for example, efforts to increase the flow of jobs to first-time teenage offenders—will (1) have unintended, difficult-to-predict side effects (or secondary impacts) which may or may not be beneficial; and (2) probably not produce the expected results, due to the continuous influence of other strands of the civicological web on the problem at hand.

Applying web theory to the problem of defining success: How, then, should one compare the success of a revitalization program that focuses narrowly but thoroughly on a small portion of the items affecting quality of life—for example, a job-creation program for teenage first-time offenders—with a program that offers assistance in many areas but at a less intense level? Although both are valuable, web theory shows that long-term revitalization is unlikely without improvement in many aspects of neighborhood life; therefore, at least theoretically, the wider the variety of quality of life measures listed above which are affected by the program, the greater the chances are that the revitalization effort will be a success.

Success for Whom?

It is possible that a project (for example, luxury housing) designed to serve groups other than low-income residents, or groups (such as customers of commercial, industrial, office, or highway developments) that may or may not include low-income residents could produce successful neighborhood revitalization. However, specific projects are deemed successful only as long as they produce improvements in the quality of life for both the new consumers and the existing low-income residents.

The massive relocation of low-income residents could be successful as well, if improvements in their quality of life were great enough to balance the destruction of the social fabric that relocation causes and if improvements were also made as promised on the site. Unfortunately, the literature clearly shows that neither of these caveats were adhered to in the urban renewal/urban highway programs, which are our most common projects involving massive relocation of the poor (Jacobs 1969; Orum 1995). There is no evidence whatsoever that this form of successful revitalization, however possible it may be theoretically, has ever actually been achieved. Therefore, in this study, the author has selected projects directly serving low-income residents.

Project Selection

The author based project selection on the following criteria:

1. Project perceived as a successful revitalization effort.

2. Project located in low-income area.

3. Project sited on government-owned property.

4. Project involved minimal displacement: either some low-income housing was provided, or the project improved both the quality of life of the surrounding area and that of the existing residents, even though it was luxury housing or nonresidential buildings.

An extensive search of revitalization project analyses produced 256 projects perceived as successful revitalization efforts. These projects, however, did not meet the other three criteria; only 98 met all four criteria. The majority of those were in the upper Midwest and Northeast. However, this does not necessarily mean that the two areas are doing a better job with low-income neighborhoods. As Greenberg and Popper (1994) found in a recent survey, "The large cities in the northeast and Midwest typically reported more TOADS than their southern and western counterparts. Buildings are newer in the Sunbelt, and the region's rapid economic growth has raised the value of almost any property in many areas" (p. 26). Since the problem is larger in the Northeast and Midwest, one would expect that they would also have the largest sampling of successful revitalization efforts.

A questionnaire was prepared to standardize data collection, and a site visit itinerary was developed. Isolated projects in less populous cities were dropped simply for logistical reasons.

Field research was conducted in eleven cities: Boston, Providence, New York, Pittsburgh, Cleveland, Chicago, Washington, D.C., Minneapolis, Seattle, Portland (Oregon), and Toronto. City staff, nonprofit group activists, and neighborhood representatives were interviewed. Interviewees were selected via a series of phone calls to find out who was most familiar with the project. In most cities, several people were interviewed; for example, five key players were visited in Seattle.

SUMMARIES OF SELECTED PROJECTS

Far more material was collected than can adequately be presented here; thus, this section will focus on the two cities that had what appeared to be the greatest success (Boston and Cleveland), followed by brief summaries of selected projects from other cities. All material was obtained during interviews with the people listed in the reference list of interviewees, unless otherwise indicated.

Boston: Dudley Street

The Dudley Street neighborhood borders the Roxbury and Dorchester sections of Boston. According to Medoff and Sklar (1994), during the 1980s, Dudley Street's largely African-American and Hispanic population had a median income of $11,750 and an unemployment rate of nearly 12.1 percent; and over 20 percent of the neighborhood had been denuded of buildings by arsonists. The neighborhood suffered dramatic population losses in the 1970s; fortunately, the remaining people were a caring core of long-time residents with deep historical roots to the community (McGuigan interview).

Over twelve hundred of these residents launched the Dudley Street Neighborhood Initiative (DSNI) in 1984 after decades of watching antipoverty agencies operate in the area with little effect. This group elected a twenty-five-member board that used a mix of public and private funds to develop a renewal plan that featured playgrounds, a central park and business district, and much rehabilitated housing.

The plan showed that the key to the neighborhood's future was to develop its vacant tax-delinquent land—this neighborhood had the highest concentration of delinquent tax land in the city. However, redevelopment was hampered by two obstacles that, incidentally, hamper reuse of delinquent tax land in every city studied. First, there were difficulties obtaining cooperation from the 130 private landowners involved. To solve this problem, the city of Boston took a very innovative step: it granted power of eminent domain over fifteen acres in the center of the neighborhood to the community leaders. The second problem involved accumulated back taxes, liens, and judgments on a considerable number of city-owned parcels, which made it uneconomical to purchase and redevelop them. The city's Public Facilities Department (which administers tax-delinquent property) solved this problem by taking another unusual step: it gave DSNI the tax-delinquent parcels to which it had already obtained title and waived all back taxes, liens, and judgments on them.

The city also subsidized the construction cost of each of the units, investing $140,000 per unit (the units sold for $90,000), most of which was due to environmental remediation costs for site cleanup. The city also provided low-interest construction financing when DSNI was unable to obtain it from lenders: even though the city put up its Community Development Block Grants (CDBG) funds as collateral, the bank still would not give a letter of credit. Ironically, DSNI was able to find permanent financing, largely due to pressure brought to bear through the Community Reinvestment Act on a bank which was seeking a merger and due to the DSNI housing director's move to a job at the bank.

This assistance allowed residents to build 38 duplex houses in 1994; Dudley Neighbors Inc. (DNI), the entity that retains ownership of the land and leases it to developers for DSNI, will soon complete construction of 50 to 60 additional units (the developers backed out, so DSNI had to take over project completion). Long-term plans call for construction of around 300 units, with total acquisition costs of approximately $2 million. Originally DSNI proposed 550 new units, but the density was reduced by 40 percent due to resident requests for yards, space, and gardens. DSNI now has a five-acre community garden and sells produce from it at the Dudley Community Market.

The support of Mayor Flynn was an important factor in getting the extensive amount of city assistance that made Dudley Street's revitalization possible. Unfortunately, not all city departments have been helpful: the public works department, for example, promised sidewalks and street improvements, but is slow in coming through.

Personal and corporate ties were also important. "We never could have done any of this without tremendous support from the legal community," said DNI's Executive Director Paul Yelder. Three big law firms gave assistance, including all the title work on the properties, the eminent domain application, all ground leases, and Ford Foundation contracts. One law firm became involved due to personal contacts with Mr. Yelder and the Riley Foundation; another attorney had been the city's corporation counsel.

The state government also helped. Under a now-defunct "town commons" program, the city received $1.5 million to develop a large pocket park-type neighborhood open space.

Paul Yelder credits the success of Dudley Street's revitalization to— among other things—the partnership between DSNI and the Riley Foundation:

> The key to Dudley's success is commitment to resident control, as can be seen from the makeup of the board. It takes longer, but it's worth it. You get a real transformation of people, a building of leadership within the community. The number of units built may not seem too impressive by CDC [Community Development Corporation] standards, but the community changes are equally, or more, important. We were fortunate to have a funder that gave us time . . . Without initial flexibility in the funding source [upfront monies for planning and startup] we wouldn't have time to go through an adequate community involvement process, especially given the city budget.

Gentrification is also a real concern, so another innovative approach was taken: Dudley Street housing is guaranteed to remain affordable via deed restrictions: namely, future buyers must be low income. The biggest roadblock, however, was having to fit into the city government's political and budget cycles and dealing with what Mr. Yelder termed the "loss of memory" that a new local administration brings.

The lesson from the Dudley Street experience: insist on a real community-led process—that is, plan to include residents in all aspects of revitalization; fund projects that are both proposed and supported by the community rather than imposed on it; and provide more flexible funds with longer time frames, particularly in the startup years.

Cleveland: Land Banking

In Cleveland, residential abandonment led to a significant TOADS problem. In the 1970s, there were about 35,000 delinquent tax parcels in Cuyahoga County, with $100 million owed in back taxes, penalties, interest, and fees. There were 16,000 vacant delinquent parcels in the city alone, with $40 million owed on them. So in the mid-1980s city officials met with the county prosecutor's office to develop a plan for reducing the problem.

The state of Ohio passed legislation in the late 1970s enabling cities to establish a Land Reutilization Authority (LRA). The city of Cleveland passed an ordinance to activate it, thus establishing the Cleveland Land Bank. The program got off to a slow start, however. Roadblocks that hampered startup included the city not really wanting inner-city land, two lawsuits that stopped the foreclosure process on fifteen thousand parcels for two years, and difficulties with the enabling legislation that allowed taxes, interest, and penalties to build up to levels that made reuse uneconomical. The law was changed in 1988, however. Now, whoever takes title must pay only the actual foreclosure costs—title, appraisal, deed, etc.—but all taxes, interest charges, and penalties are removed. Also, the county must now send the city a list of properties that are being foreclosed; the city must then return an affidavit showing each one as either "nonproductive" (vacant land not desired by the city), on the "wish list" (vacant properties, with or without structures, that the city would like to buy), or "other" (occupied homes or businesses). For the "wish list" properties, the affidavit serves as the city's bid and it will receive title if no higher bid is received. After the sale, unsold properties are forfeited to the state and then go to an annual auditor's sale. The foreclosure process takes between nine months and two years. The city also holds events such as Amnesty Week, a week in which owners can give their property to the city and all debt is forgiven.

Once a property enters the land bank, a developer may acquire it for $100; however, this does not really reflect the site cost, as buyers often face $1,400–1,500 in costs to remove the remnants of homes, contaminated soil, etc. Dates for the beginning and end of residential construction are included in the deed itself, along with a provision that the developer must pay taxes for five years. If the developer defaults on these conditions, the city can easily take back a title.

The city plan has been updated; it serves as a guide for the city's land purchases and cooperation with lenders and developers. A microplanning approach is used: planners are assigned to each of the city's neighborhoods; they (the planners) "learn all about them [the neighborhoods], lot by lot." The city's wish list is developed from these plans. "It's a proactive approach," said Nora McNamara, who works on developing neighborhood plans using land bank properties.

The city has played an important role in revitalization in many other ways, the most important being CDBG allocations to provide infrastructure, services, and rehabilitation in low-income areas. CDBG is also the largest funder of Cleveland's thirty-three CDCs. City investment of CDBG funds came before the banks were willing to invest in the neighborhoods. The city also maintains both the properties it acquires (all of which are vacant) and lots still in private hands, which cost $700–800 per lot on a current inventory of around three thousand lots. Use of these lots as community gardens is actually encouraged, as this cuts down on the city's maintenance costs. Former mayor Voinivich, mayor White, the city council, and the public were very supportive and approached the problem with a risk-taking can-do attitude.

The LRA program served as a catalyst for other development, and revitalization is now widespread despite a 40 percent poverty rate and a huge decline in population during the 1980s. LRA lots are sold for $100, low-interest financing is available thanks to Community Reinvestment Act of 1977 (CRA)-based agreements with banks along with the creation of a Housing Trust Fund, and tax abatements are also given. According to Nora McNamara, "the program made people—who previously would have rejected it—consider Cleveland as a place to live. Tax dollars are up, and there is a domino effect that attracts for-profit developers and businesses. It is very important to attract these if long-term success is to be achieved."

Central Commons, in the Hough area, is a good example of the kind of revitalization taking place. At one time 90 percent of properties in Central Commons were abandoned and tax delinquent. The lots were placed in the land bank. A consortium of foundations formed Neighborhood Progress Inc. (NPI) and its development arm, New Village Corporation. New Village Corporation offered low-cost financing to buyers of Central Commons properties. Many entities, including Habitat for Humanity, have developed homes on the once-abandoned lots. In the Glenville area, properties have been revitalized using Nehemiah grant funds. The financing used here is typical of what works in low-income areas. The city sells the lots from its land bank for $100 each; local banks provide low-interest first mortgages; and a city program provides second and third mortgages but their repayment is deferred and, if the owner stays for 8 years, waived. Taxes are abated for seven to fifteen years on the building, and private foundations provide grants to lower the cost further. The result is a total payment of $475 per month by the owner for a very nice home.

The extent of the city's success is shown by the fact that when interviewees were asked what their biggest roadblock is, they answered "multiple bidders on the delinquent properties"—a new phenomenon that seems to be a measure of increased demand. This also means that the city is having difficulty acquiring all the properties it wants. Thus, plan implementation is suffering.

The LRA idea did not originate in Cleveland; Saint Louis was the first city in the nation to establish a land bank for government-owned property. Now several cities in Ohio, including Dayton, Youngstown, Columbus, and Toledo, also have them.

According to Michael Sweeney, director of the county delinquent tax department, there are several lessons to be learned from the Cleveland experience: "Emphasize detailed (lot and block level), proactive planning with extensive community input, and a multiyear program—

more than three years—with funds for acquisition so they can make things happen within a reasonable time. This is attractive to developers, too. Federal funds are absolutely critical. [CDCs are important, but] you must have community consensus, and you must get private dollars to kick in." Finally, city-county cooperation is needed.

New York: Advance and Retreat

New York has by far the largest property abandonment/city acquisition program of any city visited, and contains the largest number of successful revitalization projects. According to professor Alex Schwartz:

> Tax-foreclosed property (in-rem) has been integral to the city's housing and neighborhood development activities. The city has helped finance the development and rehabilitation of more than 150,000 units of housing, at a cost exceeding $3 billion since 1986. Most of this activity involves vacant and occupied buildings and lots, mostly located in a handful of neighborhoods such as the South Bronx, which has been completely rebuilt because of the city's housing program. In general the city transfers these properties to nonprofit groups at a nominal cost along with low-interest loans for renovation. Sometimes these projects also receive low income housing tax credits. (1996)

New York is a city of neighborhoods, so there are many CDCs in place, and many of these have recycled tax-delinquent city-owned property in the South Bronx, the Upper West Side, and Brooklyn.

Ironically, the city has decided to stop foreclosing on tax-delinquent property and is making a concerted effort to liquidate its remaining inventory. Interviewees attribute this change to a combination of high maintenance costs, lack of developer interest, and loss of political support. Thus, although New York has probably achieved more success at recycling city-owned properties than any other city, the enormous magnitude of the problem has prevented these efforts from turning the tide of abandonment and has engendered new city policies that will worsen the situation.

The biggest roadblock is a lack of funds. The Federal Government (HUD) could help by (1) providing more funds along with more tax breaks, (2) assisting with grassroots organization, (3) forming CDCs for project management, and (4) making sure that ideas come from and are supported by the residents. Leonard Hopper, the Housing Authority's chief landscape architect, finds that "it is especially important to provide federal funds for new construction of low-income housing, which is not profitable enough for private developers to provide. Now, new construction is mixed income (one-third low-moderate, one-third low, and one-third public assistance) and this does not work for developers."

Pittsburgh: CRA at Work

TOADS, especially tax-delinquent properties, are an enormous problem in Pittsburgh, due in part to the city's 50 percent population loss over the past twenty years. There are thousands of delinquent lots. The nonprofit organizations have formed a Vacant Property Working Group (VPGW) to deal with this issue. They are looking at changes in state laws (which govern treasurers' sales in "second-class" cities), city policies (which appear to be causing much trouble), and prevention programs. The city has a program to transfer delinquent lots to adjacent owners for $125 or so. However, other types of reuse are difficult because there is no database, and all charges remain on the properties until they have already been through the treasurer's sale and have been foreclosed (at which point all debts are wiped out). Still, the VPWG is developing a plan for about one hundred tax-delinquent homes.

The main roadblock in Pittsburgh was the capacity of community groups to locate funds, organize, lobby, etc. Staff turnover needs to be lowered, and the staff should be professionally trained. The groups also need more resources and they need to do more strategic planning.

Providence: Too Many Cooks?

The city of Providence had record unemployment; it was a city of empty, crumbling buildings. Patrick McGuigan, director of the Providence Plan, feels that Providence and other New England cities have a large tax-delinquency problem because there is a population outflow, so the land market is poor. About 400–450 tax title lots have been recycled for use as gardens, homes, etc. in Providence, but there are also more than 700 vacant abandoned buildings in the city, so there is still a big problem. According to Matthew Powell, director of Providence Plan Housing Corporation (PPHC), Providence inner-city areas suffer from a byzantine delinquent tax auction process, poor record-keeping, and an "old boys network" of slumlords. The result is that not much land is actually city-owned, and that which the city does own consists mainly of vacant, old commercial buildings or very dilapidated housing.

PPHC gets the first opportunity to buy delinquent tax property being offered at the tax sales, but they must pay all back taxes, fees, etc. The PPHC organization is older than the Providence Plan organization and is a citywide nonprofit corporation, but is heavily controlled by the mayor—so banks and community groups are suspicious of it. There are many other groups trying to address the problem, but the mayor and business community have focused their attention on downtown, so neighborhood efforts have been fragmented.

The Federal-DePasquale project, named after a street intersection, is in an area characterized by tiny lots and huge homes with big families. It was originally Italian but is now experiencing in-migration of African Americans and Latinos. In 1991 many credit unions were shut down due to the failure of their guaranteeing agencies. The city took over forty mainly vacant properties in a two-acre area which contained ninety-six dwelling units and four commercial structures. They obtained a Nehemiah (HUD) grant that allowed them to offer "soft second" financing of $15,000, cleared the area, replatted it into twenty-one lots, and gave the land to the new owners. The owners would then get a mortgage and build as follows: $75,000 price – $15,000 soft second – $15,000 given by the state = $45,000 mortgage.

Blackstone, named after a wealthy street in another part of town, began revitalization when the city bought 23 lots (phase 1), 11 lots (phase 2) and 15–20 lots (phase 3), mainly vacant. Again, Nehemiah funds were used. Since these allow for no administrative costs, the city provided staff. PPHC is doing prequalification and development; the city is doing paving, trees, acquisition, and demolition. The homes will sell from $75,000 to $80,000 each. Also, the city has helped Interfaith Housing rehabilitate several rental buildings using city-owned properties around town; SWAP (Stop Wasting Abandoned Property) is now revitalizing a block with a city gift of the land; the mayor formed a Vacant Lands Task Force, which has introduced changes in state legislation which would emphasize planning, reuse of abandoned homes, use of vacant lots for community gardens, etc.; and the South Side Community Land Trust is using tax-delinquent lands for community gardens. Tax-delinquent land must be sold for "fair market value," but the city says that if a nonprofit agency plans to develop it, that value is one dollar.

"Housing has been the stepchild of government, and poor areas are very capital-intensive. Cities must have some incentive to make a long-term commitment to invest X dollars each year, and integrate code enforcement, rehabilitation, and other physical revitalization programs,"

1. The biggest roadblocks to success are the lack of regular investment in housing, and lack of a comprehensive program of physical revitalization.

City Planner Thomas Deller would advise HUD to provide funds with fewer strings attached, and not targeted for the poorest parts of town because these require much more funding and effort. The city should also focus its efforts on transitional neighborhoods; then when they are fixed, "we can move backwards" to the worst areas, rather than doing projects in every ward, as is the case now.

Seattle: Beyond Pike Place

Delinquent tax land is not much of a problem in Seattle. The demand for housing is strong, property values are rising, and many homes throughout the city are valued at over $125,000. However, Seattle has had its share of troubles in trying to reuse, successfully, property that fell into government hands for a variety of other reasons. As neighborhood planner George Frost said, "There is no place where property is unsaleable, but there is land that the state took."

Pike Place Market is a well-known downtown revitalization project; less well known is the associated reuse of this and nearby property, acquired by the government during the urban renewal program, for low-income housing. The redevelopment was spearheaded by the Pike Place Public Development Authority (PDA), which set out to rebuild 700 units of low-income housing, about half of which were already vacant. There are now over 500 low-income units, above the Pike Place shops or within two blocks of the urban-renewal area. A few market-rate units were also provided by the PDA; there are now more than 400 market rate units in the area. Pike Place is much more than a housing or retail project. Pike Place also includes a free medical clinic, a child and adult day care center, and a food cooperative. All of these entities have nonprofit boards under the PDA (which operates much like a CDC), and are operated by PDA using its "surplus cash flow." It is now "a mixed-use, mixed-income neighborhood which has made a dramatic comeback over the past twenty years," according to PDA's first executive director, George Rolfe.

The Judkins-Rejected area is a less successful revitalization effort. In the 1940s the federal government dug a tunnel for I–90; it also acquired considerable land both above and around the tunnel, but this land was underused and some areas were even abandoned. Thus, decline in the Judkins-Rejected area was caused by I–90 (interview with Janeen

Smith). Beginning in 1984, however, the state of Washington rebuilt and expanded the I–90 tunnel; the state also acquired more property that was later purchased by the city of Seattle.

Homesight, a community-based nonprofit corporation, has built many units of single family and duplex housing in Seattle over the past four years, some of which utilized the I–90 surplus land. The city made $1.5 million available to Homesight for assistance to low- and moderate-income first-time buyers. Homesight also obtained a Nehemiah Housing Opportunity Program grant to provide $15,000 interest-free equity loans. Average home cost is $125,000, which is covered by a $90,000 mortgage and $35,000 in housing assistance (the Nehemiah mortgage plus city and state assistance). So far 55 homes are completed, of which 29 are in the I–90 area under discussion; the rest are in other parts of central and southeast Seattle. Homesight's goal is to complete 100 units in 1997; by then, it is hoped that the area will have improved sufficiently enough for revitalization to proceed through the private market.

CONCLUSIONS

TOADS Must Be Recycled

Interviewees repeatedly cited the ability to recycle TOADS as the single most critical factor in achieving their goals. This perception is borne out by the fact that those projects which were most widely recognized as successful (and which appeared to be most successful in the site visits)— Boston, Cleveland, and some New York projects—had all been able to reuse most of these properties. They achieved this goal by acquiring properties at a very low cost and with minimal legal hurdles. Without this ability other revitalization efforts do not succeed well, as seen in Pittsburgh, Providence, and much of New York.

Problems often stemmed from the fact that some state laws and local policies regarding property appraisal and/or resale are blatantly discriminatory against low-income areas. For example, appraisal techniques based on comparable sales can produce very high tax bills if applied to areas where the property is not listed with realtors and is ineligible for mortgages. Appraisal techniques based on averaging within a geographic area clearly subsidize the wealthy and penalize the poor. Laws requiring a minimum bid that approaches a property's market value make government-owned land unattractive to developers and nonprofits alike. According to Marino, Rosser, and Rozran (1979):

In many communities (the delinquent tax property disposition system) is a poor method for preventing neighborhood deterioration due to abandonment. First, . . . property on sale for taxes is not very attractive to potential buyers since debts secured by the property (i.e., mortgages and mechanic's liens) are transferred along with the title and become obligations of the new owner (and, this author would add, since they are often conveyed by quit claim deed, the government makes no promises regarding existence of these liens—it is up to the buyer to obtain a title search). Second, properties not sold early in the delinquency cycle become less likely to be purchased in successive years since each year adds another year's worth of back taxes to the major rehabilitation . . . To maintain a neighborhood's attractiveness, strategies should be developed by local governments to acquire tax-delinquent properties from owners who are maximizing short-term profit (by not paying taxes) at the expense of the surrounding neighborhood (p. 19).

States and localities interested in inner-city neighborhood revitalization should begin with a hard look at the appraisal, collection, forfeiture and resale practices governing delinquent tax properties, and the legal and financial restrictions surrounding the reuse of other TOADS. Changes in these laws and policies may be needed before successful revitalization can occur.

Residents Must Be in Charge

Area residents know what they need far better than anyone else, and they also have extensive knowledge of the local urban web upon which microplanning must be based. The path through which this seems to have occurred in the most successful revitalization efforts begins with a charismatic leader or several leaders organizing the neighborhood, sometimes with the assistance of a faith-based organization—for example, the archdiocese in Pittsburgh. Soon, this organization becomes a CDC or similar entity. Here is where serious problems are likely to occur due to the need for capacity-building: It is difficult to find interim funding to get thoroughly organized and truly involve the residents. Robert Washington, professor of urban studies at the University of New Orleans, commented in a recent speech (October 4, 1996, UNO library): "Community-based organizations (CBOs) are short-lived in poor neighborhoods. They need good long-range capacity-building, not just charismatic leaders." In the successful efforts, corporate foundations usually filled this important gap.

Recycling TOADS Is Not Enough

All major strands of the urban web that determine the quality of life in low-income areas must be addressed. Many examples of this multifaceted approach have been discussed in this study. Changing a few strands of the web in hopes of revitalizing the area dooms the entire revitalization effort to failure, and may even create a situation where different levels of government or even departments within the same level are sabotaging each others' efforts. Reusing TOADS is a good beginning, but other aspects of the web must be integrated if revitalization is to succeed.

Table 3–2
Apparent Commonalities of Successful Projects

• Successful reuse of TOADS
• Resident direction for the entire effort, usually through CDCs
• Residents developed programs to address a wide spectrum of problems
• Presence of a local "champion" to lead revitalization efforts, especially in startup years
• Initial funding from altruistic corporate foundation (Riley, Casey, McKnight, Ford, LISC, etc.) or church
• Detailed, lot-by-lot "microplanning" done by residents with city and sometimes university help
• Use of CRA to force lender participation
• Some assistance from private business—for example, free legal work
• Strong mayoral support, city staff support (CDBG allocations, etc.), and voter support
• State support in resolving many issues, including liability issues stopping brownfields redevelopment; creative financing for low-income buyers; provision of park land; making bank deposits in community banks; eliminating barriers to TOADS redevelopment; etc.
• Regional cooperation was often present and took many forms, including cooperative TOADS reuse programs, tax-base sharing, cooperation among boroughs, growth management, and regional provision of infrastructure and transit
• Federal funds were very important, especially CDBG, Nehemiah, HOPE, and HOME
• Federal tax credits were an important incentive for developers/investors

RECOMMENDATIONS

In designing a national program or in allocating funds, HUD and other levels of government should give primary importance to the following:

I. Foster participation by developers, lenders, and other corporations in inner-city neighborhood redevelopment. The most glaring "missing player" in the case studies is the private for-profit business sector. This might be due to the extreme difficulty of making a profit in inner-city redevelopment; it is a very high-risk venture.

    A. Provide more direct financing; that is, shift risk from the private to the public sector, and include measures taken at the national level to encourage more voluntary lender activity (perhaps FHA and VA loan programs could serve as models).

    B. Strengthen the Community Reinvestment Act, and change other national-level barriers to obtaining loans in transitional, low-income, mixed-use neighborhoods.

    C. Review federal regulation on assisting the private sector to shoulder risk.

    D. Develop mechanisms to make funding available for the startup years of community-based organizations. Seattle and Cleveland provide models that may prove useful here, although a greater private sector presence would be desirable.

II. Foster citywide and regionwide policies to support inner-city revitalization efforts, not undermine them.

    A. Encourage development of regionwide support mechanisms for inner-city revitalization (for example, tax-base sharing, strict growth management).

    B. Cities, in particular, need to reexamine the effect of their zoning ordinances and code enforcement practices on revitalization efforts. For example, a poor ordinance may needlessly restrict accessory apartments but allow noxious uses.

    C. Cities, in collaboration with lenders and developers, need to provide services such as land assemblage and title transfer. The partnerships developed for downtown revitalization projects may serve as models for establishing these partnerships.

D. Provide a full spectrum of municipal services. If the city government is unwilling to invest heavily in ensuring that services such as trash collection, transit, child care, medical services, alcohol/drug treatment, are available, then beautification or physical rehabilitation efforts will produce very limited revitalization success. As Professor Clarence Stone of the University of Maryland said (speech, October 4, 1996, UNO library), "The future of the city depends on its public facilities. [For example] you can't restore the city's economic health without restoring its schools."

Currently, the burden of providing these falls disproportionately on nongovernmental organizations, and sometimes services are even withheld from these neighborhoods until residents become organized enough to demand the same levels of service that wealthier areas are given. The case studies show that cities have voluntarily become active when conditions became so bad that the voters were demanding something be done (working through their CBOs), and when a mayor was elected with a strong interest in redevelopment.

III. Additionally, interviewees made the following suggestions:

- Insist on a community-led process for all aspects of revitalization, from development of initial ideas through construction.

- Help with grassroots organization, CDC formation, and capacity building, including developing professional skills in obtaining funds, lobbying, etc.

- Require detailed lot and block "microplanning," and strategic planning.

- Provide more flexible funds with fewer strings attached and longer time frames (more than three years), especially in the startup years.

- Make funds available for transitional neighborhoods rather than focusing on the poorest parts of town, where success is more costly and less likely.

- Provide more direct funding for acquisition and construction of low-income housing, in addition to tax shelters.

REFERENCES

Action-Housing, Inc. 1996. *Status report on housing development activities 1986–1996.* Pittsburgh, PA: Unpublished report (July).

Adler, William M. 1995. *Land of opportunity: One family's quest for the American dream in the age of crack.* New York: Atlantic Monthly Press.

Allen, W. and A. Mckinnon. 1979. Development pays off in Newark. Commentary, *National Council for Urban Economic Development, 8:* 3–6 (October).

Alterman, Rachelle. A comparative view of neighborhood regeneration programs in nine countries: Are the lessons transferable? *Urban Affairs Review, 30*(5): 794–765 (May 1995).

Alterman, Rachelle and Goran Cars, eds. 1991. *Neighbourhood regeneration: An international evaluation.* New York: Mansell Publishing.

American Public Health Association Committee on the Hygiene of Housing. 1947. *Planning the neighborhood.* New Haven, CT: American Public Health Association Committee on the Hygiene of Housing.

Anderson, Donnie, Dristin Hadawi, and Alaeddin Shuroro. 1995. *Healthy communities project: a plan for economic health for the near north side neighborhood.* Center for Economic Development Research and Service Report 95–96 (Spring). Arlington, TX: School of Urban and Public Affairs, University of Texas at Arlington.

Anderson, Elijah. 1990. *Streetwise: Race, class, and change in an urban community.* Chicago: University of Chicago Press.

Andrew, Christine I. and Dwight H. Merriam. 1988. Defensible linkage. *APA Journal.* American Planning Association (Spring).

Anonymous. 1967. *Go ask Alice.* New York: Prentice-Hall, Inc.

Babcock, Richard and Clifford Weaver. 1979. *City zoning: The once and future frontier.* Chicago: Planners Press.

Bailey, Laura. 1995. Proposal for the City of Houston Planning Department. *Planning & Development Department.*

Baker, Keith. 1995. *Evaluating small scale community based programs.* Washington, DC: The Milton S. Eisenhower Foundation.

Barrett, Katherine and Richard Greene. 1993. Pittsburgh: Trickling up. *Financial World, 162*(5): 54–55 (March).

Baum, Alice S. and Donald W. Burnes. 1993. *A nation in denial: The truth about homelessness.* Boulder, CO: Westview Press.

Baumgartner, M. P. 1988. *The moral order of a suburb.* New York: Oxford University Press.

Begovich, Ray. 1995. From Blight to Bright: The transformation of an entire block. *Journal of Housing & Community Development, 52*(5): 21–23 (September).

Bernick, Michael. 1996. Transit villages: Tools for revitalizing the inner city. *Access.* Berkeley: University of California Transportation Center.

Birch, Eugenie. 1996. Planning in a world city: New York and its communities. *Journal of the American Planning Association* No. 4 (Autumn).

Blakely, Edward J. 1994. *Planning local economic development: theory and practice.* Thousand Oaks, CA: Sage Publications.

Blue Hill Avenue Task Force. 1996. *Blue Hill Avenue . . . a community vision.* Boston: Blue Hill Avenue Task Force.

Bogdon, Amy S. and James R. Follain. 1996. Multifamily housing: An exploratory analysis using the 1991 residential finance survey. *Journal of Housing Research* Vol. 7 Issue 1.

Bright, Elise M. 1995. *Taking without compensation in low-income areas: Turning tragedy into opportunity.* Center for Economic Development Research and Service Report 95–13 (August). Arlington, TX: School of Urban and Public Affairs, University of Texas at Arlington.

Bright, Elise, et al. 1996 *Economic asset and community development plan for the near southeast neighborhood: Ft. Worth, Texas.* 1996. Arlington, TX: City and Regional Planning, University of Texas at Arlington.

Bureau of Governmental Research. 1992. *Inventory of economic development programs in the city of New Orleans, 1970–1992:* Working Paper No. 2 (September). New Orleans: National Center for the Revitalization of Central Cities.

Bursik, Robert J. Jr. and Harold G. Grasmick. 1993. *Neighborhoods and crime: The dimensions of effective community control.* New York: Lexington Books.

Burton, Dorothy, Pete Meador, and John Warren. 1987. *Community revitalization in South Dallas/Fair Park.* Arlington, TX: School of Urban and Public Affairs, University of Texas, Arlington.

Byrum, Oliver. 1992. *Old problems in new times: Urban strategies for the 1990s.* Chicago: American Planning Association.

Cervero, Robert. 1996. Jobs-housing balance revisited: Trends and impacts in the San Francisco Bay area. *Journal of the American Planning Association.* No. 4 (Autumn).

City of Chicago. 1996. *Cityspace: An open space plan for Chicago.* Chicago: City of Chicago.

Clapp, James A. 1971. *New towns and urban policy.* New York: Dunellen Publishing Company, Inc.

Clark, Thom. 1985. Housing After Section 8: Coping with the cuts. *The Neighborhood Works.* Vol. 8 No. 1 (January).

Cleveland City Planning Commission. 1991. *Cleveland civic vision 2000 citywide plan.* Cleveland: Cleveland City Planning Commission.

Clinton, Hillary Rodham. 1996. *It takes a village: And other lessons children teach us.* New York: Simon and Schuster.

Coffey, Brian and Nancy Kleniewski. 1988. New houses on old lots. *Planning.* Vol. 7 (September).

Cole, Richard L., Ann Crowley Smith, and Delbert A. Taebel. 1984. *The quality of life in Texas cities: A ranking and assessment of living conditions in Texas' largest communities.* Arlington, TX: Institute of Urban Studies.

Committee for Economic Development. 1982. *Public-private partnerships: An opportunity for urban communities.* New York: Committee for Economic Development.

Community Action Program. 1967. *It's your neighborhood.* Washington, DC: U.S. Printing Office, p. 1.

Cook, James. 1987. Priming the urban pump. *Forbes, 139*(6): 62, 64. (March).

Craig, W. 1983. The second coming of Newark. *New Jersey Reporter,* p. 19–23 (September).

Department of Community Development. *Cleveland's field of dreams.* Cleveland: Deptartment of Community Development.

Detroit City Planning Department. 1995. *Detroit empowerment zone.* Detroit: Detroit City Planning Department.

Dillon, David. 1988. A Downtown Success Story: Kansas City brings housing back to a historic district. *The Dallas Morning News,* pp. 1c, 3c.

Division of Neighborhood Services. 1996. *Year 22 block grant council briefing document.* Cleveland: Department of Community Development.

Edmondson, Brad. 1986. The Midwest: St. Paul's American beauty. *American Demographics.* Vol. 8 No. 5., pp. 44 (May).

Elias, C. E. Jr., James Gillies, and Svend Riemer. 1966. *Metropolis: values in conflict.* Belmont, CA: Wadsworth Publishing Co., Inc.

Enterprise Foundation. 1995. *A time of change: 1995 annual report.* Columbia, MD: The Enterprise Foundation.

Environmental Protection Agency Office of Research and Monitoring Environmental Studies Division. 1973. *The quality of life concept: A potential new tool for decision-makers.* Environmental Protection Agency.

Everybody's Money. 1977. Sweat equity pays off. *Everybody's Money.* (Summer).

Fainstein, Susan S. 1994. *The city builders.* Cambridge, MA: Blackwell Publishers.

Feagin, Joe R. and Robert Parker. 1990. *Building American cities: The urban real estate game.* Englewood Cliffs, NJ: Prentice-Hall, Inc.

Federation of Tax Administrators. 1984. *The discovery and collection of delinquent taxes: A compilation of state programs and procedures.* Research report no. 101.

Fitzparick, Dan. 1996. What happened to . . . The hill district?. *Minority Business Times.*. Supplement to the Pittsburgh Business Times. (July 1).

Fleming, Ronald Lee. 1994. Saving face: How corporate franchise design can respect community identity. *Planning Advisory Service Report* 452 (June). Chicago: American Planning Association.

Ford Foundation. 1973. Community development corporations: A strategy for depressed urban and rural areas. New York: Ford Foundation.

Frieden, Bernard J. 1990. Center city transformed: Planners as developers. *Journal of the American Planning Association* 56.

Frieden, Bernard J. 1995. The urban policy legacy. *Urban Affairs Review, 30*(5): 681–686 (May).

Frieden, Bernard J. and Lynne B. Sagalyn. 1992. Downtown, inc.: *How America rebuilds cities.* Cambridge: The MIT Press.

Fuller, Millard and Linda Fuller. 1990. *The excitement is building: How Habitat for Humanity is putting roofs over heads and hope in hearts.* Dallas: Word Publishing.

Gans, Herbert J. 1962. *The urban villagers: Group and class in the life of Italian Americans.* New York: Free Press of Glencoe.

Gilderbloom, John I. 1993. A new lease on life for rent control. *The Wall Street Journal,* p. A11 (August 19).

Gilderbloom, John I. 1995. Rebuilding Russell: Rebirth of a Louisville neighborhood. *CUPR Report* Vol. 6 No. 3/4, p. 5.

Gilderbloom, John I. and Mark T. Wright. 1993. Empowerment strategies for a low income African American neighborhood. *Harvard Journal of African American Public Policy,* pp. 77–95.

Gilderbloom, John I. and R. L. Mullins, Jr. 1995. The university as a partner for rebuliding an inner city neighborhood. *Metropolitan Universities,* pp. 79–95 (Winter).

Glaser, Mark, Kathryn Denhardt, and Joseph Grubbs. 1995. *Critical partnerships and community organization: Local government intervention and the formation of a community-based organization.* Portland, OR: Urban Affairs Association paper. (May).

Gould, Jay M. 1986. *Quality of life in American neighborhoods: Levels of affluence, toxic waste, and cancer mortality in residential zip code areas.* Boulder, CO: Westview Press.

Gratz, Roberta Brandes. 1994. *The living city: How America's cities are being revitalized by thinking small in a big way.* Washington, D.C.: The Preservation Press.

Gratz, Roberta Brandes. (1995).The Preservationist. *Town and Country.*

Greenberg, Michael R., and Frank J. Popper. 1994. Finding treasure in TOADS. *Planning.* (April.)

Gruen, Victor. 1964. *The heart of our cities: The urban crisis diagnosis and cure.* New York: Simon and Schuster.

Gunsch, Dawn. 1993. Urban renewal is an investment. *Personnel Journal, 72* (3): 53–55.

Harayda, Janice. 1995. Sober view of the city: Essays say Cleveland has much work ahead. *CUPR Newsletter.* New Jersey: Council for Urban Planning Research, Rutgers University (October 15).

Hare, Patrick H., Susan Conner, and Dwight Merriam. 1981. Accessory apartments: Using surplus space in single-family houses. *Planning Advisory Service Report* 365 (December). Chicago: American Planning Assn.

Henry, J. Marilyn. 1996. NAHRO awards of excellence. *The Journal of Housing and Community Development,* Vol. 53 No. 1 (Jan./Feb.).

Hill, Lewis W. and Frankie M. Boylan. 1972. A housing rehabilitation program. *Planners Notebook.* American Institute of Planners. Vol. 2 No. 3 (June).

Hinshaw, Mark L. 1995. Design review. *Planning Advisory Service Report* 454 (February). Chicago: American Planning Assn.

Horowitz, Craig. 1994. South Bronx renaissance. *New York.* (November).

Housing and Neighborhood Development Division. 1992. *Erie-Ellington neighborhood partnership initiative.* Boston: Public Facilities Department.

Howe, Deborah A., Nancy J. Chapman, and Sharon A. Baggett. 1994. Planning for an aging society. *Planning Advisory Service Report* 451 (April). Chicago: American Planning Association.

Howington, Patrick. 1993. Home fair for first-time buyers offers hope, draws a crowd. *The Courier-Journal,* p. B3 (August 22).

Hoyle, Cynthia L. 1995. Traffic calming. *Planning Advisory Service Report* 456 (July). Chicago: American Planning Association.

Ian, Harris. 1986. New owners replace absentees. *The Neighborhood Works,* pp. 27–28 (January).

Imbroscio, David, Marion Orr, Timothy Ross, and Clarence Stone. 1993. *Baltimore and the human-investment challenge.* Working Paper No. 5 (February). New Orleans: National Center for the Revitalization of Central Cities.

Jacobs, Jane. 1969. *The economy of cities.* New York: Vintage Books.

Judd, Dennis and Michael Parkinson. 1990. *Leadership and urban regeneration: cities in North America and Europe.* Newbury Park, CA: Sage Publications.

Kaufman, Tracy. 1996. Poverty housing defeats families. *Habitat World.* Vol. 13 No. 1 (Feb/Mar).

Kearns, Gerry and Chris Philo, eds. 1993. *Selling places: the city as cultural capital, past and present.* New York: Pergamon Press.

Keating, W. Dennis, Norman Krumholz, and David C. Perry, eds. 1995. *Cleveland: A metropolitan reader.* Kent, OH: Kent State University Press.

Kleniewski, Nancy. 1997. *Cities, change, and conflict: A political economy of urban life.* Belmont, CA: Wadsworth Publishing Company.

Knox, Paul L. 1995. Book review—Breakthroughs. Re-creating the American City (by Neal R. Peirce and Robert Guskind). *Economic Geography, 71*(3): 335–336 (July).

Kupel, Jim. 1984. Portland, Maine, grows through cooperative effort. *American City & County,* p. 74 (November).

Lake, Robert W. 1979. *Real estate tax delinquency: Private disinvestment & public response.* New Brunswick, NJ: The Center for Urban Policy Research.

Lane, Vincent. 1995. Best management practices in U.S. public housing. *Housing Policy Debate.* Washington, DC: Office of Housing Research, Fannie Mae.

Lang, Michael H. 1982. *Gentrification amid urban decline: Strategies for America's older cities.* Cambridge: Ballinger Publishing Company.

Lauria, Mickey, Robert K. Whelan, and Alma H. Young. 1993. *Urban revitalization strategies and plans in New Orleans, 1970–1993.* Working Paper No. 10 (April). New Orleans: National Center for the Revitalization of Central Cities.

Levitt, Rachell L., ed. 1987. *Cities reborn.* Washington, DC: Urban Land Institute.

Linnen, Beth. 1989. "Hard-headed do-gooders" drive the redevelopment of Chicago's South Side. *Savings Institutions.* (February).

Local Initiative Support Corporation. 1996. *Celebrating the campaign for communities and fifteen years of revitalizing America's neighborhoods.* New York: LISC.

Loukaitou-Sideris, Anastasia and Tridib Banerjee. 1996. There's no there there: Or why neighborhoods don't readily develop near light-rail transit stations. *Access.* Berkeley: University of California Transportation Center.

Lunt, Penny. 1993. Urban allies on the move. *ABA Banking Journal, 85*(8): 34–42 (August).

Lurcott, Robert H. and Jane A. Downing. 1987. A public-private support system for community-based organizations in Pittsburgh. *JAPA,* pp. 459–468.

Marino, Dennis R., Lawrence B. Rosser, and Andrea R. Rozran. 1979. The planner's role in facilitating private sector reinvestment. *Planning Advisory Service Report* 340 (March). Chicago: American Planning Association.

Martz, Wendelyn A. 1995. Neighborhood-based planning: Five case studies. *Planning Advisory Service Report* 455 (March). Chicago: American Planning Association.

Matulef, Mark Lewis 1986. Focus on Chicago. *Journal of Housing.* (Sept./Oct.).

McKee, Bradford. 1995. South Bronx. *Architecture—The AIA Journal, 84*(4): 86–95 (April).

McKenna, Linda. 1988. Working partnership. *Mortgage Banking.* (July).

McNulty, R.J. et al. 1985. *The economics of amenity: community futures and quality of life.* Washington, DC: Partners for Livable Places.

Mead, Lawrence M. 1992. *The new politics of poverty.* New York: Basic Books

Medoff, Peter and Holly Sklar. 1994. *Streets of hope: The fall and rise of an urban neighborhood.* Boston: South End Press.

Mellon Bank Corporation. 1995. *1995 community report: Our changing communities.* Pittsburgh: Mellon Bank.

Metzger, John T. *The Community Reinvestment Act and neighborhood revitalization in Pittsburgh.* Albany, NY: SUNY Press.

Mier, Robert. 1993. *Social Justice and Local Development Policy.* Newbury Park, CA: Sage Publications.

Mills, Steven. 1986. Bank contributions to community investment corp. help rejuvenate run-down Chicago neighborhoods. *American Banker.* Vol. 151 (January).

Millstein, David L. and John J. Hopkins. 1987. Hatching opportunities. *Real Estate Today,* pp. 76–78 (October).

Moore, Donnie L. 1992. *1992 Sandbranch annexation feasibility study.* Arlington, TX: City and Regional Planning—University of Texas at Arlington. (Unpublished report).

Muhammad, Lawrence. 1994. Applied academics: Louisville professor John Gilderbloom takes his theories of social activism to the streets. *Planning,* pp.16–19 (May).

National Trust for Historic Preservation. 1992. *Using the Community Reinvestment Act in low-income historic neighborhoods.* Washington, DC: National Trust Historic Preservation.

Nelson, Arthur and Jeffrey H. Milgroom. 1993. *The role of regional development management in central city revitalization: Case studies and comparisons of development patterns in Atlanta, Georgia, and Portland, Oregon.* Working Paper No. 6 (April). New Orleans: National Center for the Revitalization of Central Cities.

Netzer, Dick. 1972. *Economics of the property tax.* Washington, DC: The Brookings Institution.

Newton, Patrina L. 1994. *Retail potential in the stop six neighborhood.* Arlington, TX: City and Regional Planning—University of Texas at Arlington. (Unpublished report)

Office of University Partnerships. 1995. *University-community partnerships: Current practices.* Rockville, MD: U.S. Department of Housing and Urban Development.

Oldman, Oliver and Henry Aaron. *Assessment—sales ratios under the Boston property tax.* National Tax Journal Vol. XVIII.

Olsen, Susan and M. Leanne Lachman. 1983. *Tax delinquency in the inner city.* New York: McGraw Hill.

Olson, Christopher. 1985. St. Paul revives an urban village. *Building Design & Construction.* Vol. 26 No. 2.: 63–66 (February).

Orum, Anthony M. 1995. *City-building in America.* Boulder, CO: Westview Press.

Osborne, David and Ted Gaebler. 1993. *Reinventing government: How the entrepreneurial spirit is transforming the public sector.* New York: Plume.

Page, Clint. 1982. Urban progress depends on grassrooots talent. Small business can rise or fall on local factors. *Nation's Cities Weekly* (January 11).

Page, Clint. 1984. Corporate leadership in urban redevelopment. *Nation's Cities Weekly.* Vol. 7 (February 13).

Paine, Sylvia. 1995. Treasured Island. *Minneapolis St. Paul 23*(10): 62–63. St. Paul, MN.

Patton, Michael Q. 1993. *The Aid to Families in Poverty program: A synthesis of themes, patterns and lessons learned.* Minneapolis, MN: The McKnight Foundation.

Peirce, Neal R. 1995. Redeveloping a city—The smart way. *National Journal, 27*(37): 2304 (September)

Peirce, Neal R. 1995. How a city finally found its way. *National Journal, 27*(13): 826 (April).

Peirce, Neil R. 1983. How women may remake face of American city. *Nation's Cities Weekly* (August).

Peirce, Neal R. 1985. Renewing an inner city and retaining historic character. *Nation's Cities Weekly,* Vol. 8. (July).

Peirce, Neal R. 1982. Urban progress depends on grassrooots talent. Center promotes new policy for neighborhoods. *Nation's Cities Weekly* (January 11).

Perry, Stewart. 1987. *Communities on the way: Rebuilding local economies in the United States and Canada.* Albany: State University of New York Press.

Phillips, E. Barbara. 1996. *City lights: Urban-suburban life in the global society.* New York: Oxford University Press.

Pittsburgh Community Reinvestment Group. 1995. *Follow the money: Neighborhood lending report 1991–1994.* Pittsburgh: Pittsburgh Community Reinvestment Group.

Podolefsky, Aaron and Fredric Dubow. 1981. *Strategies for community crime prevention: Collective responses to crime in urban America.* Springfield, IL: Charles C. Thomas.

Pogge, Jean. 1985. *From obstacle to opportunity: An evaluation of the multifamily tax reactivation program.* Chicago: Woodstock Institute.

Pratt Institute Center for Community and Environmental Development. 1992. *Uprooting poverty through community development.* Brooklyn: Pratt Institute Center for Community and Environmental Development.

Providence Plan Housing Corporation. 1995. *Rebuilding Providence.* Providence, RI: Providence Plan Housing Corporation.

Providence Plan Housing Corporation. 1996. *Rebuilding Providence: A report to the board of directors for calendar year 1995 activity.* Unpublished report (January).

Rayburn, Kevin. 1993. No room at the inn. *ET Ultra* (Winter/Spring).

Reardon, Kenneth M. *Institutionalizing community service-learning at a major research university: The case of the East St. Louis Action Research Project.* Unpublished paper.

Rogers, Mary Beth. 1990. *Cold anger: A story of faith and power politics.* Denton, TX: University of North Texas Press.

Rogowsky, Edward T. and Ronald Berkman, project directors. 1993. *New York's "Outer Borough" development strategy: Case studies in urban revitalization.* Working Paper No. 8 (April). New Orleans: National Center for the Revitalization of Central Cities.

Rooney, Jim. 1995. *Organizing the South Bronx.* Albany: State University of New York Press.

Rosen, David. 1987. Housing trust funds. *Planning Advisory Service Report* 406 (December). Chicago: American Planning Association.

Rothschild, Jan. 1996. South Bronx comprehensive community revitalization program. *Planning.* Vol. 62 No. 4 (April)

Roudebush, Janice and Leslie J. Well. 1980. Low- and moderate-income housing: Part I. Increasing the supply and accessibility. *Planning Advisory Service Report* 350 (May). Chicago: American Planning Association.

Roudebush, Janice, and Leslie J. Well. 1980. Low- and moderate-income housing: Part II. Conserving what we have. *Planning Advisory Service Report* 351 (June). Chicago: American Planning Association.

Rubin, Debra K. 1989. Blighted cities rise from the ruins. *ENR Market Focus* (May).

Saffrin, Joni and Alan Goldberg. 1985. Cities reclaim SRO housing. *The Neighborhood Works* (September).

Saltman, Juliet. 1990. *A fragile movement: The struggle for neighborhood stabilization.* Westport, CT: Greenwood Press.

Savageau, David. 1993. *Places rated almanac: Your guide to finding the best places to live in North America.* New York: Prentice Hall, Inc.

Sawicki, David S. and William J. Craig. 1996. The democratization of data: bridging the gap or community groups. *Journal of the American Planning Association* No. 4 (Autumn).

Schein, Virginia E. 1995. *Working from the margins: Voices of mothers in poverty.* Ithaca, NY: Cornell University Press.

Schulgasser, Daniel M. 1989. *Urban revitalization in Newark, New Jersey: from the core to the periphery of the issue.* Unpublished paper (March).

Singer, Karen. 1989. A reborn Providence turns to face a bright future. *Adweek's Marketing Week* (January)

Sommerfeld, Meg. 1993. In Baltimore, residents, foundation lift a "sinking" community. *Education Week, 12*(38): 10–11 (June).

Squires, Gregory D. 1994. *Capital and communities in black and white: The intersections of race, class, and uneven development.* New York: State University of New York Press.

State of Rhode Island and the City of Providence. 1994. *Nomination for Providence, Rhode Island designation as an enterprise community.* Report (June).

Stern, Jennifer. 1989. Pratt to the rescue: Advocacy planning is alive and well in Brooklyn. *Planning, 55*(5): 26–28 (May).

Stone, Clarence. 1996. Speech delivered at National Center for the Revitalization of Central Cities seminar, Earl K. Long Library, University of New Orleans. October 4.

Sutro, Suzanne. 1990. Reinventing the village: Planning, zoning, and design strategies. *Planning Advisory Service Report 430* (December). Chicago: American Planning Association.

Swartz, Alex. 1996. Personal correspondence with author.

Taub, Richard P., D. Garth Taylor, and Jan D. Dunham. 1984. *Paths of neighborhood change: Race and crime in urban America.* Chicago: University of Chicago Press.

Teitler, Andrea. Not in my neighborhood: Urban gentrification. *Crisis, 102*(4): 31–32 (May).

Temkin, Kenneth and William Rohe. 1996. Neighborhood change and urban policy. *Journal of Planning Education and Research* No. 3 (Spring).

Third Ward Redevelopment Council (1995). *Greater Third Ward Community Plan.* Houston, TX: City of Houston.

Thomas, Jim. 1985. Dallas groups finding housing "common ground." *The Neighborhood Works.* (January.)

Thomas, Tina N. 1996. *Redevelopment plan for Joppa: A model plan for dilapidated, low-income minority neighborhoods.* Arlington, TX: City and Regional Planning—University of Texas at Arlington. (Unpublished report submitted to the school of Urban and Public Affairs, August.)

Urban, Jim. 1996. Do or die: Can we resuscitate the region? *Executive Report* (January).

U.S. Department of Education. 1994. *Youth and tobacco: Preventing tobacco use among young people.* Washington, DC: Department of Health and Human Services.

U.S. Department of Housing and Urban Development. 1995. *Empowerment: A new covenant with America's communities.* Washington, DC: U.S. Department of Housing and Urban Development.

van Vliet, Willem and Jan van Weesep, eds. 1990. *Government and housing: developments in seven countries.* Newbury Park, CA: Sage Publications.

Varady, David P. 1986. *Neighborhood upgrading: A realistic assessment.* Albany: State University of New York Press.

Vardey, Lucinda. 1995. *Mother Teresa: A simple path.* New York: Ballantine Books.

Vergara, Camilo Jose. 1995. Downtown Detroit: An American Acropolis. *Planning.* Vol. 61, No. 8 (August)

von Hoffman, Alexander. 1994. *Local attachments: The making of an American urban neighborhood 1850 to 1920.* Baltimore: Johns Hopkins University Press.

Wagner, Fritz, Timothy E. Joder, and Anthony J. Mumphrey Jr., eds. 1995. *Urban revitalization: Policies and programs.* Thousand Oaks, CA: Sage Publications.

Waldsmith, Lynn. 1995. 400 homes for Detroit part of $46-million plan. *The Detroit News,* p.1A, 8A (October 20).

Wallace, James E. 1995. Financing affordable housing in the United States. *Housing Policy Debate.* Washington, DC: Office of Housing Research, Fannie Mae.

Washington, Robert. 1996. Speech delivered at the National Center for the Revitalization of Central Cities Seminar, Earl K. Long Library, University of New Orleans. October 4.

Weisman, Leslie Kanes. 1992. *Discrimination by design: A feminist critique of the man-made environment.*Chicago: University of Illinois Press.

Wekerle, Gerta and Carolyn Whitzman. *Safe cities: Guidelines for planning, design, & management.* New York: Van Nostrand Reinhold.

Whelan, Robert K., Alma H. Young, and Mickey Lauria. 1993. *Urban regimes and racial politics: New Orleans during the Barthelemy years.* Working Paper No. 7 (January). New Orleans: National Center for the Revitalization of Central Cities.

Wilson, David. 1987. Urban revitalization on the Upper West Side of Manhattan: An urban managerialist assessment. *Economic Geography.* Vol. 63 No. 1 (January).

Wilson, William J. 1987. *The truly disadvantaged: The inner city, the underclass, and public policy.* Chicago: University of Chicago Press.

Wurtzel, Elizabeth. 1995. *Prozac nation.* New York: Riverhead Books.

Young, John A. 1988. Richmond study focuses on downtown housing needs. *Nation's Cities Weekly.* (January 25.)

Zimmer, Jonathan E. 1977. *From rental to cooperative: Improving low and moderate income housing.* Professional Paper. Beverly Hills, CA: Sage Publications.

LIST OF INTERVIEWEES

Boston

Paul Yelder, executive director, Dudley Neighbors Incorporated
Michael Thomas, planner, Neighborhood Planning, Public Facilities Department

Cleveland

Nora McNamara, planner, City of Cleveland
Michael M. Sweeney, director, Delinquent Tax Department, Office of the County
    Treasurer
Joseph A. Sidoti, assistant commissioner, Department of Community Develop-
    ment, City of Cleveland
Kate Monter Durban, assistant to the director, Cleveland Housing Network

Minneapolis/St. Paul

Earl Pettiford, housing manager, MCDA
Dawn Hagen, MCDA
Jennifer Billig, Neighborhood Revitalization Program, MCDA
Lawrence Soderholm, principal planner, City of Saint Paul
Gary Peltier, housing administrator, City of Saint Paul

New York

Donald C. Burns, planner, Bureau of Planning and Development, Bronx
Takisia L. Ward, urban planner, Bureau of Planning and Development, Bronx
Leonard J. Hopper, chief, landscape architecture section, New York City Housing
    Authority
Several people at the Local Initiatives Support Corporation (LISC)
Several people at the Enterprise Foundation
Several people at the Pratt Institute for Community and Economic Development

Pittsburgh

Aggie Brose, Bloomfield-Garfield CDC
Rhonda Brandon, executive director, Manchester Citizens Corporation
Myron Dowell and others at the Pittsburgh Community Reinvestment Group
    (PCRG)
John Zimmer, director, Action Housing

Providence

Patrick McGuigan, executive director, The Providence Plan
Matthew Powell, executive director, PPHC
Thomas E. Deller, deputy director, Department of Planning and Development
Hilary Silver, associate professor of sociology and urban studies, Brown University

Seattle

George Rolfe, professor, University of Washington
George W. Frost, project manager, Neighborhood Planning Office, City of Seattle
Patricia J. Chemnick, economic development manager, Southeast Effective Development
Ruby Jones, director, UCEDA CDC
Several employees, CADA CDC
Mike Usen, planner, city of Seattle
Janeen Smith, project manager, Housing Development and Rehabilitation Unit, Seattle Department of Housing and Human Services
Mark Pomeroy, Housing Development and Rehabilitation Unit, Seattle Department of Housing and Human Services
John Burbank, Fremont Public Association

CHAPTER 4

Managing Development in New York City: The Case of Business Improvement Districts

EDWARD T. ROGOWSKY AND JILL SIMONE GROSS

Local economic development policy, in general, refers to an urban policy the goal of which is the creation of jobs and wealth that are directed at strengthening the local tax base and enhancing local economic opportunity.

Traditional approaches to economic development in American cities have been undertaken by a host of actors and organizations. Working in concert to revitalize depressed older downtowns, which are often the most visible signs of urban decay, this multiactor approach, which brought together federal, state, and city funds, reflected more centralized development strategies. These projects made extensive use of federal funds—Community Development Block Grants (CDBGs) and Urban Development Action Grants (UDAGs)—but they were for the most part designed and managed by local governments, with active participation from private interests.

Over the past several decades America's older downtowns have experienced significant decline. This is explained in part by the following factors: decline in the federal resources going to urban centers; flight of middle-class populations from the central cities to the suburbs; and the relocation of central city retailers to suburban shopping malls. In response to this predicament, central cities have pursued new development schemes and public–private partnerships. These new forms—in contrast to traditional centralized development strategies—are characterized by a greater reliance on local initiation, participation, and decentralized decision-making (Bennett, 1994).

In this context, public—private partnerships have become common techniques of urban economic development (Squires, 1991). They are partnerships in the sense that actors representing both public and private sector interests work together in pursuit of urban revitalization goals, though the balance of power and initiative within the partnership varies. Most often, local governments take on the role of "underwriter." City governments entice businesses to either remain in or relocate to downtown areas by offering tax abatements and other financial incentive packages. A more recent manifestation of the partnership is the Special Assessment District (SADs) or Business Improvement District (BIDs).[1]

Business improvement districts represent a particular form of partnership between city government and local property owners. The initiative for a business improvement district may come from a variety of groups: local property owners, merchants, local development corporations, or chambers of commerce; and in the case of New York City, from a community board, a borough president, or a mayoral agency. However, once officially designated, decision-making within the business improvement district is dominated by private property owners who finance the partnership through a mutually agreed upon supplementary property tax assessment.

In contrast to the traditional government—sponsored tax abatement methods, business improvement districts represent tax increases sponsored by the property owners. The public component of this partnership takes the form of government as a facilitator and oversight agent, while the private sector controls and manages daily BID activities.

Problem Definition

This study focuses on the business improvement district as an agent of local economic development. In the past, urban economic development efforts were based upon the notion of a "field of dreams," which implied "if you build it they will come." However, city government, planners, and business and economic development experts have increasingly begun to recognize that after "you build it" and "they come," you must then generate capacity in the downtown to keep the existing businesses there, attract new business, and keep shoppers coming back. Economic revitalization, therefore, requires more than simply rebuilding the physical infrastructure: it also requires a strategy for maintaining current activities and developing an organizational structure that can maintain these investments and their viability as sites for ongoing investment.

This study analyzes the role of one particular type of organizational structure—the business improvement district. Our goal is (1) to describe and analyze the structure and function of business improvement districts as agents of economic development, and (2) to draw inferences that might inform subsequent BID development in New York City and in other central cities.

What follows is a discussion of urban economic development and business improvement districts based on the history and current experiences of four business improvement districts in two of New York City's outer boroughs, Brooklyn and Queens. Through in-depth interviews with BID administrators, local development experts, community organizations, and government officials and a survey of BID users, we examine the effectiveness of business improvement districts to deliver services (e.g., security, sanitation, and infrastructure maintenance) and promote the area.

Because business improvement districts occupy small areas for which quantitative economic indicators are not readily available, we developed qualitative measures based on field research and the perceptions of BID actors (i.e., property owners, tenants, merchants, consumers, city and state officials).[2] Specifically, data were drawn from two primary sources:

- *BID Creators:* In-depth interviews were carried out with BID managers (both past and present), city officials, local development experts, city planning officials, federal development officials, and local business leaders (see References for full interview list).
- *BID Users:* Consumer intercept surveys were carried out in each BID (a total of 350 individuals were surveyed as to their perceptions of cleanliness, security, shopping, and amenities in the BID area, and the degree of change that they have seen over time.

National Perspective

Business Improvement Districts are "self-taxing/self-help groups" in which the property owners agree to pay additional taxes on their properties. This additional tax is then collected by the city and returned to a BID management association for the provision of services above and beyond those already provided by the municipality. Currently there are over one thousand business improvement districts nationwide, with thirty-nine in New York City alone (New York City Department of City Planning, February 1996).

Most states have some form of BID enabling legislation. While the scope and sophistication of the services vary, all business improvement districts have as their common goal the improvement of the economic and business environment.

Property owners, merchants, and tenants within the BID, in conjunction with agents of city government, enter into a jointly created contractual arrangement. The contract identifies a range of services to be provided by the BID within a geographically defined area. Funding for these services is derived from the mutually agreed upon additional property tax. In a 1995 *Urban Land* article, "Betting on BIDs," Lawrence Houstoun Jr. commented on the several key elements that are common to most business improvement districts:

- The initiative comes from business leaders who seek common services beyond those that the city can provide.
- The city determines boundaries, approves the annual budget and the financing strategy, and determines what services may be provided.
- Business leaders shape the annual budget, hire staff, let contracts, and generally oversee operations. (1994)

The size of business improvement districts varies nationally, from small shopping districts with small budgets to major business centers with multimillion-dollar budgets.

Despite the proliferation of business improvement districts nationally, there has been little substantive analysis of the effectiveness of business improvement districts as agents of economic development. New York's city government has long been an advocate of BID/SAD partnerships in support of urban revitalization efforts (it sanctioned its first SAD in 1976). Subsequently it has been at the forefront of BID creation and development. As one city official commented, "officials from other cities come to look at us." New York is the model (Barbara Wolff interview, August 1996):

> Business improvement districts are now almost ubiquitous in New York City, encompassing such disparate pieces of urban geography as the Upper East Side, the Lower East Side, Brighton Beach, and the East Brooklyn Industrial Zone. Other, often struggling commercial districts in the city are clamoring for BID status, and the New York BID model is being replicated from Chicago to Philadelphia to Los Angeles to San Francisco (Jacobs and Saffro, 1996).

Typology of Business Improvement Districts

Business improvement districts do not fall into one discrete category. Based on our investigation and analysis of BIDs both nationally and locally, we propose the following typology: corporate, main street, and community.

The Corporate BID. There are only ten corporate BIDs in New York City, eight of which are in Manhattan. These business improvement districts are dominated by large commercial property owners, have budgets over one million dollars, and contain large amounts of office space and retail space. The Grand Central Partnership in Manhattan, for example, covers 54 square blocks (71 million square feet of commercial, retail and hotel space in the central business district). A significant proportion of the partnership's budget, in excess of $9 million, is used for services such as security, sanitation, maintenance, merchandising, and social services for the homeless. Beyond the provision of these basic services, corporate BIDs also spend monies on capital improvements to public spaces.

One of the country's oldest and perhaps largest corporate business improvement districts is in New Orleans: the Downtown Development District was created in 1975. It covers a two hundred-block area and has a budget of roughly $3.5 million. This BID provides services such as sanitation, security, capital improvements, and marketing. Yet another corporate BID, located in Philadelphia, is the Philadelphia Center District BID (started in 1991). It covers an eighty-block area and has a budget of roughly $7 million. The BID provides sidewalk cleaning, marketing, and supplemental security. Corporate business improvement districts generally develop in wealthy areas of the central city. Corporations, in developing these BIDs, seek to maintain and improve the physical infrastructure in support of their presence. In a recent *City Journal* article, McDonald commented on the Grand Central Partnership "BID taxes are virtually the only taxes in the city [that are] spent locally; those who pay more get more. . . . Certain areas of the city are economically more important than others." (p. 42)

After official approval by the city government, these corporate business improvement districts, by virtue of their extensive resources and expertise, operate with a great degree of independence from city and local community interests. As a result, according to John Beam (1995), "business improvement districts are sometimes criticized for using their tax-supported organizational clout to push problems out into the surrounding community" (p. 35).

Corporate business improvement districts have been highly successful as supplementary service providers. For example, "property owners . . .
point to the existence of the BID to explain the zero vacancy rates in
many of buildings" (MacDonald 1996, p. 40). The success of corporate
BIDs, however, is not surprising because these develop in the more affluent sections of cities. Of the ten corporate BIDs in New York City, eight
are located in Manhattan; six of the eight are found in those sections of
Manhattan with the highest assessed commercial property values. These
six have a combined budget in excess of $25 million.

The Main Street BID. In contrast to their corporate counterparts,
the main street business improvement districts are smaller, both economically and programmatically. There are eighteen main street BIDs in New
York City. These business improvement districts cover between five and
twenty square blocks, and their budgets range from $200,000 to $1 million. Main Street BIDs develop in those parts of a central city's downtown where retail and commercial businesses have left for the suburbs.
These businesses have primarily followed the flight of middle-class families to the suburbs. Thus, the socioeconomic base has also changed in
those downtown areas; it is characterized by new immigrant populations
and the working poor. The main street BID is also more typical of most
business improvement districts nationwide than the corporate or community type BID. In New Jersey, all six of its business improvement districts
are of the main street type.

While people with managerial expertise and business acumen occupy the organizational structure and membership of corporate BIDs,
main street BIDs are less likely to have individuals with managerial expertise, financial resources, and access to government. According to John
Beam of the New York City Economic Policy and Marketing Group:

> Small business improvement districts spend two and a half times more
> of their budget on administration than large business improvement dis-
> tricts . . . because small business improvement districts . . . are . . . less
> able to take advantage of economies of scale in administration. . . . In
> addition, large business improvement districts prepare more sophisti-
> cated budgets (May 1995, p. 14).

The role of "main street" business improvement districts is complex.
First, this type of BID needs to unify an often fragmented business community; second, it must garner support from existing property owners
with diverse interests; and third, the BID must attract new investors into
areas that have suffered visible physical, economic, and social decline.

These business improvement districts also become involved with re-defining the downtown such that it accommodates the new immigrant community, with a lower yet stable economic presence.

The Community BID. Community business improvement districts are the smallest of the BIDs. Community BIDs are found in both wealthy and poor areas, although they are more common in poorer economic environments. They often exist on fewer than three blocks. The community BID's budget is typically less than $200,000. Eleven of New York's business improvement districts fall in this category, but there are only two in Manhattan.

The community—type business improvement district covers an area from a single block to a small shopping strip. According to Barbara Wolff, assistant commissioner of New York's Department of Business Services, most community BIDs developed from earlier neighborhood shopping strip/commercial revitalization projects that were funded from CDBG allocations. These districts offer limited sanitation services and intermittent promotional activities such as holiday lighting and decoration.

Our study examines each of these three BID types: corporate, main street, and community. Specifically, we look at the role of four business improvement districts in two of New York's outer boroughs: the Metro-tech business improvement district, which is a corporate BID; and the Fulton Mall special assessment district, which is a main street BID. Both are located in Brooklyn. The Jamaica Center business improvement district, which is a main street BID, and the 165th Street Mall, which is a community BID, are located in Queens. Our conclusions are drawn from the four case studies, intercept surveys, and personal interviews.

NEW YORK CITY'S BUSINESS IMPROVEMENT DISTRICTS

Historically, assessment districts in New York were used for limited infrastructure repairs, such as road improvements, the creation of better sewer systems, and to implement other public purpose programs. During the mid 1970s, New York City established special assessment districts (SADs) as a means to finance the maintenance of renewed downtown infrastructures (i.e., roads, streets, sidewalks, etc.). In the late 1970s, special assessment districts were replaced by the business improvement district. These districts were also responsible for managing public spaces (i.e., shopping malls, shopping strips, plazas, streetscapes, etc.).

The technical difference between the special assessment district and the business improvement district rests in their legal origin. Special

assessment districts were individually established through site specific state legislation. Business improvement districts, on the other hand,
are created by the municipality. Under this more generic state law, all
municipalities were empowered to establish business improvement districts.

In New York city the budgets for business improvement districts
range from $65,000 to $9 million. This wide range comes from the
types of services provided, the type of property (commercial or industrial), and the owners involved. Over the past decade, business improvement districts have taken on a variety of economic development roles
because of local desires to assure that previous investment is supported
by an economically viable commercial area. All business improvement
districts seek to improve the economic and business environment of
their constituents.

Business improvement districts enable local property owners and
merchants in retail, commercial, and industrial areas to provide services
that supplement those already provided by the city. At the same time,
some have questioned whether city agencies reduce their expenditure for
those services voluntarily provided by the BID. This has led to questions
regarding the degree to which the public-private combination is actually
a partnership between business improvement districts and the city government. This district, however, is not meant to replace the city as the
basic service provider, but rather to supplement it.[3]

The role of city government in business improvement districts is
most pronounced during the approval stage. City government, in partnership with local communities, determines the boundaries, approves the
annual budget and financing strategy, and determines what services a
district may provide. Once approved, the property owners, business leaders, and merchants shape the annual budget, hire staff, let contracts, and
oversee daily operations.

The initiative to form a business improvement district comes from
local property owners, merchants, or civic organizations; although, city
officials often suggest BID formation in conjunction with funding for
specified city projects. In New York City, the establishment of business
improvement districts is supervised by the Department of Business Services. The Department requires extensive community outreach during
the planning process. This process is designed to build consensus among
owners, tenants and residents, the community boards, city council representatives, and other elected officials. If a majority (51 percent) of the
property owners object to establishing a business improvement district,
then the proposal fails. However, in the absence of a majority objection

then the proposal is passed on to New York's city council for its approval—that is, the council must adopt local legislation creating the business improvement district. Following city council adoption, it must be signed into law by the mayor, who then submits an application to the New York State comptroller for final review and approval.[4]

Business improvement districts in New York are managed by a nonprofit corporation designated for each area, the District Management Association (DMA). Funds are collected by the city and then returned to the association for its use. Day-to-day operations are carried out by the association, which is a public-private partnership with four classes of membership: property owners, commercial tenants, residential tenants, and city officials. Property owners must make up a majority of the district management association's board of directors. At a minimum the board must include seven property owners, one residential tenant, one commercial tenant, a local city councillor, and representatives from the mayor's, city comptroller's, and borough president's offices. Community boards are represented as nonvoting members. District management associations in New York City have as few as thirteen members and as many as fifty members.

New York City is a pioneer in creating special assessment districts and business improvement districts. The city had four special assessment districts in operation by the late 1970s, and it currently has thirty-nine business improvement districts in operation and many more in the planning stages (see Figure 4–1).[5]

The budgets of the city's business improvement districts ranges from $65,000, in the case of the Grand Street BID in Brooklyn, to $9 million, in the case of the Grand Central Partnership in Manhattan. Business improvement districts in Manhattan have budgets that are roughly ten times greater than the budgets of districts in the other boroughs.

Another difference between the Manhattan business improvement districts and those in the outer boroughs has to do with their origins. For the most part, business improvement districts in Manhattan never received the influx of federal monies that the outer borough areas did. Manhattan's business improvement districts were the product of corporate interest and financed by corporate dollars. In most cases they were not eligible for federal community development monies, because they were well beyond "poverty levels."

Finally, Manhattan business improvement districts are much more involved in economic development (marketing, area promotion, and capital improvements) than the outer borough BIDs (See Tables 4–1 and 4–2).

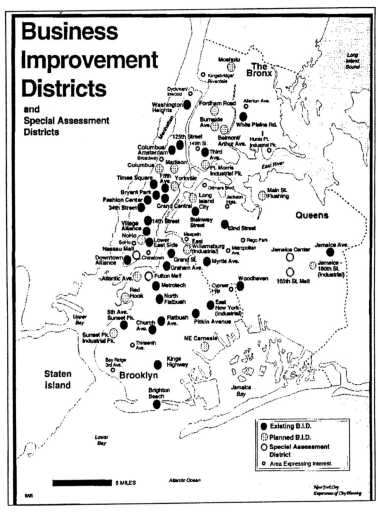

Figure 4–1. Business Improvement Districts and Special Assessment Districts

Sources: New York City Department of Business Services (June, 1996); New York City Department of Business Services (August, 1995)

Table 4–1.

BOROUGH	BID NAME	BUDGET (in $)
Brooklyn	Brighton Beach	150,000
	Church Avenue	110,000
	East Brooklyn	310,000
	Flatbush	250,000
	Fulton Mall	980,000
	Graham Avenue	115,000
	Grand Street	65,000
	Kings Highway	150,000
	MetroTech	1,800,000
	North Flatbush	82,500
	Pitkin Avenue	105,000
Queens	82nd Street	130,000
	Jamaica Center	600,000
	Myrtle Avenue	222,000
	165th Street	169,000
	Steinway Street	223,000
	Woodhaven	160,000
Bronx	HUB—3rd Avenue	260,000
	White Plains Road	67,000
Manhattan	Bryant Park	950,000
	Columbus—Amsterdam	168,000
	Downtown Lower Manhattan	8,650,000
	Fashion Center	3,000,000
	Fifth Avenue	1,800,000
	14th Street	794,000
	Grand Central	9,000,000
	Lower East Side	200,000
	Nassau St. Mall	198,000
	125th Street	275,000
	34th Street	6,300,000
	Times Square	4,650,000
	Village Alliance	476,000
	Washington Heights	205,000

Sources: New York City Department of Business Services (June, 1996);New York City Department of Business Services (August, 1995); New York City Department of Business Services (July, 1995).

Table 4–2
Services Provided by Business Improvement Districts in New York City

Borough	Bid Name	Security	Sanitation	Promotion	Holiday	Capital	Marketing	Graffiti	Maintenance	Info.
Brooklyn	Brighton Beach		*	*						
	Church Avenue	*	*			*				
	East Brooklyn	*								
	Flatbush	*	*	*						
	Fulton Mall	*	*	*		*				
	Grand Street			*	*					
	Kings Highway	*	*	*	*			*		
	MetroTech	*	*	*			*			
	North Flatbush	*	*		*		*		*	
	Pitkin Avenue	*		*	*					
Queens	82nd Street		*		*		*			
	Jamaica Center		*							*
	Myrtle Avenue		*		*		*			*
	165th Street		*	*			*		*	
	Steinway Street	*	*	*	*					
	Woodhaven	*	*	*						

Borough	Bid Name	Security	Sanitation	Promotion	Holiday	Capital	Marketing	Graffiti	Maintenance	Info.
Bronx	HUB—3rd Avenue	*	*	*	*					
	White Plains Road		*							*
Manhattan	Bryant Park	*	*			*	*			
	Columbus–Amsterdam		*	*						
	Downtown Lower Man.	*	*	*						
	Fashion Center	*	*			*	*			
	Fifth Avenue	*	*							
	14th Street	*	*	*						
	Grand Central	*	*	*		*				
	Lower East Side		*	*						
	Nassau St. Mall	*	*		*					
	125th Street	*	*	*						
	34th Street	*	*	*		*				
	Times Square	*	*	*						
	Village Alliance	*	*	*						
	Washington Heights		*	*	*					

Broad Description of what Types of Services Are Included in Each Category: Security—provision of guards, surveillance cameras, community watch, etc. *Sanitation*—supplementary crews, sidewalk sweepers, snow removal, etc. *Promotion*—Newsletters, events, shopping guides, etc. *Holiday*—Special lightings and decoration. *Capital*—Physical improvements, that is, facade, street light replacement, tree planting. *Marketing*—services to attract buyers. *Graffiti*—graffiti removal, power washing. *Maintenance*—Maintenance of sidewalks, brick replacement, bench painting, etc. *Info.*—provision of information for tourists, shoppers, etc.

Sources: New York City Department of Business Services (June, 1996); New York City Department of Business Services (August, 1995); New York City Department of Business Services (July, 1995).

CASE STUDIES: BROOKLYN AND QUEENS

Downtown Brooklyn and Jamaica, Queens, share many common features and experiences—both have a history of thriving commercial activity, both include major transportation hubs (commuter rail, bus, and subway), and both were major entertainment centers. In recent decades, however, Queens and Brooklyn have undergone a basic transformation in their population bases (ethnically, racially, and economically). Both have struggled to survive as vital commercial, retail, and business centers in the face of changing trends and national economic downswings.

Up until the opening of the Brooklyn Bridge in 1883, Brooklyn's downtown area was home to the only ferry connecting Brooklyn and Manhattan. As such, it was Brooklyn's main shopping, cultural, education, commercial, and civic center. Likewise, the Jamaica area of Queens occupied a central location between Manhattan and suburban Long Island, and has long been an area of economic significance.

Both areas have historically been home to national department stores, major universities, local government offices, city services, and a host of other businesses. The areas are also central transportation hubs with multiple subway lines, a host of bus routes, and the Long Island Commuter Railroad. Thus, these areas were thriving business centers for the boroughs of Brooklyn and Queens.

Between 1950 and 1970, the areas began to decline, largely due to the movement of white working- and middle-class populations to the suburbs, particularly to Long Island and Westchester County. These suburbs also attracted retailers and shoppers away from downtown. As population and retail declined, the boroughs also lost their local newspapers and banks, and witnessed the exit of manufacturing industries.

In the late 1960s business and civic leaders in each borough began to explore mechanisms to stem downtown decline. While these groups shared common problems in both boroughs, the mechanisms they adopted to respond to their challenges and the partners involved differed.

In Jamaica, civic and business leaders joined forces with the Jamaica Chamber of Commerce, leading ultimately to the formation of two special assessment districts: Jamaica Center and the 165th Street Mall. Fulton Mall, a special assessment district in downtown Brooklyn, originated with a partnership among local business and civic leaders and the borough. Metrotech, also located in Brooklyn, emerged from a partnership among a private university (the Polytechnic Institute), a property developer (Forest City Enterprises), the borough president, and other city agencies.

Brooklyn's Fulton Mall

In late 1967, a group of Brooklyn's downtown business people met to explore what could be done to save the area from further decline. The Downtown Brooklyn Development Association was created out of that meeting. The group took on an advocacy role for the community. It appealed to city agencies to give downtown Brooklyn a higher priority among the city's other development requests. In 1971, due to the efforts of the Downtown Brooklyn Development Association, the mayor's Office of Downtown Brooklyn Development (ODBD) was established. Two years after that organization's creation, the Fulton Mall Arcade was proposed. The proposed arcade would upgrade and modernize Fulton Street and thus help stem economic decline. The redevelopment plan was based upon the emerging suburban "mall" phenomenon. Specifically, the redevelopment plan involved creating an integrated and accessible urban shopping area with amenities designed to enhance the physical space. This design, in theory at least, would increase local pedestrian traffic, which in turn would increase retail activity and thus revitalize downtown Brooklyn. Barbara Wolff, assistant commissioner of the New York City Department of Business Services (DBS) recalls:

> I think if anything, the nationwide increase of shopping malls and managed shopping centers was an incentive to give these neighborhood areas the desire to do something similar. The need to compete with safer, cleaner, managed, organized and not just physically improved shopping areas. (DBS Focus Group Meeting)

In 1977, after extensive planning efforts and funding appeals, Fulton Mall became a reality. Financing for the project came from an Urban Mass Transportation Administration (UMTA) Capital Improvement Grant. The Fulton Mall project converted Fulton Street into an eight-block pedestrian shopping area with limited vehicular traffic. As part of the redevelopment, the following aesthetic and functional changes were made:

1. Narrow roadway.
2. Buses only.
3. Delivery trucks restricted to nonshopping hours.

4. Larger sidewalks.
5. Street repaved.
6. Decorative brick crosswalks.
7. Kiosks, telephones, light poles, water fountains, directories, bus shelters, trees, and benches.

During this time there was also a shift in thinking on the part of city officials: major public investments would require long-term commitments from the local business community. Barbara Wolff explains:

> Part of the deal as regards the initial investment to rebuild [Fulton Street] was an agreement that these communities would also arrange to maintain the developed areas after.

The Fulton Mall Improvement Association (FMIA) was formed in 1976 out of the Fulton Mall Committee of the Downtown Brooklyn Development Association.[6] This association's role was to administer and provide services within the Fulton Mall special assessment district. The association is composed of the nearly 130 retail and other business owners whose stores stand along Fulton Street (FMIA: Winter 1979).

Brooklyn's Metrotech

Metrotech is a more recent development; it was established in 1992. While planning for the Metrotech facility began in the 1980s, the area had been designated for urban renewal as early as the 1960s. No revitalization plans were adopted until the dominant property holder in the area, the Polytechnic Institute of New York (PINY), threatened to leave. Polytechnic officials approached the city with a request to upgrade their Brooklyn campus:

> Inspired by the success stories of research and development meccas built around MIT in Cambridge and Stanford in Silicon Valley, PINY officials had the idea of creating a high—tech research center around the downtown Brooklyn campus. (Rogowsky et al. 1995, p. 87)

While city officials were supportive of the concept, they were skeptical about Polytechnic's capacity to develop and manage a large-scale project with significant public financial risk. In conjunction with the city's Public Development Corporation, Polytechnic began an outreach program that resulted in the selection of Forest City Ratner as a development partner. The Metrotech partnership leveraged their joint interests into a formal plan and a request for city support in their development efforts. The Metrotech project received $71 million in public funds (two UDAG grants totaling $14 million; $30 million from the city; $3 million in low interest industrial revenue bonds; a $14 million loan from the Port Authority of New York/New Jersey; and a $10 million loan from the Municipal Assistance Corporation). The city also provided a range of tax rebates and tax credits.

Unlike Fulton Mall, where city agencies instigated the creation of a special assessment district to manage public investments, in Metrotech it was the corporate investors themselves who initiated the process to create a business improvement district that would manage the area.

While Fulton Mall extends for eight blocks, Metrotech covers a twenty-five block area (about sixty acres); traffic is restricted within the twenty-five block area. The geographic heart of Metrotech is known as the "Commons." It is a high-tech office and educational complex that is home to Chase Manhattan Bank, Brooklyn Union Gas, the Securities Industries Automated Corporation (SIAC), and the Polytechnic Institute. These corporate anchors surround a 3.3 acre park. Surrounding the "Commons" are two universities; a Bell Atlantic telephone facility; city, state, and federal agencies; and retail and service establishments. At its fringes, Metrotech has an older retail corridor comprised of small and often transitory retailers. This corridor existed prior to the construction of the Metrotech facility, and it is now the focus of redevelopment efforts by the business improvement district.

Queens: Jamaica Center and the 165th Street Mall

In contrast to Brooklyn's business improvement districts, Queens' Jamaica's districts share one historical beginning and two subsequently diverging paths. The players in Jamaica's redevelopment were a combination of local organizations and private interests. The key actors included the Greater Jamaica Development Corporation (GJDC), the Jamaica Chamber of Commerce, and the major property owners along Jamaica Avenue.

Public investment in Jamaica—especially between the late 1960s and early 1980s—was considerable. However, unlike the Brooklyn downtown experience, physical redevelopment in Jamaica lacked a coherent focus; redevelopment occurred in a piecemeal fashion. For example, in 1973 the elevated subway line running over Jamaica Avenue was removed to enhance the physical appearance of the avenue. Fifteen years later, that former elevated rail line was replaced with underground subway lines. Between 1974 and 1986, City University built its York College campus in the area. In 1978, the 165th Street Mall was completed. In 1987 the federal government completed the building of a new regional headquarters for the Social Security Administration. As in the case of Fulton Mall (a main street BID), the city—to protect its various investments in Jamaica—promoted the idea of a special assessment district. Two districts were ultimately formed: the 165th Street Mall, a "community"-type BID, was established in 1978; and Jamaica Center, a "main street" BID, was established in 1979.

The 165th Street Mall was created to manage the upkeep of a shopping strip. The intent was to lure back shoppers who had been attracted to the suburbs. This mall is a three-block shopping strip similar to many suburban shopping mall areas. The mall includes decorative brickwork, benches, and trees, and all vehicles are restricted. The mall, however, suffered an immediate setback when, upon its completion, it lost its largest property owner, a Macy's department store, which had been considered a vital attraction and financial base for the district.

The Jamaica Center district was an outgrowth of the 165th Street Mall. The separation had to do with differences in the types of property in Jamaica Center. The objective of this new district was to retain and redevelop commercial office and retail space on Jamaica Avenue. Interviews revealed that the city lacked confidence in the capacity of the 165th Street district to oversee development on Jamaica Avenue.

Although the districts remained distinct and separate entities, they both contracted with the Jamaica Chamber of Commerce to provide services. This relationship lasted until 1994. Barbara Wolff comments, with regard to Jamaica:

> The BID role in the early years was strictly service provision, and it was really just the Chamber of Commerce that ran things. They still focus on the small stuff.

One motive for utilizing the Chamber of Commerce in this role related to its historic ties to local business people in Jamaica. According to Jerry Gertz, a long-standing property owner in the area:

> The Chamber of Commerce . . . was used in conjunction with the BID District. So the concept at the beginning was that, in order to have the Chamber of Commerce survive, the work of the BID would be done by the Chamber, which would bill the expenses to the BID.

The relationship among the small business and property owners in both districts proved to be highly contentious. The in-fighting between BID members ultimately resulted in poor district management and inadequate service provision in both business improvement districts. In 1994, the relationship formally ended when a court—supervised election installed a new board of directors at the Jamaica Center SAD and discharged the Jamaica Chamber from its managerial role. The Chamber remained the District Management Association for the 165th Street Mall. Much of the contention related to the alleged misappropriation of BID funds by the Chamber. Both business improvement districts are currently involved in litigation concerning this breakup.

Since 1994, the business improvement districts have been run as separate entities, each with its own management team. The differences are stark. As field visits revealed, Jamaica Center shows visible signs of improvement (new signage, new stores, colorful decorations, and city-wide promotion of the area in various media) while 165th Street recedes into further decay (dirty sidewalks, broken paving stones, and several storefront vacancies). Jamaica Center has attracted new retailers and chain stores, while 165th Street remains a series of small businesses, many of which are troubled.

ASSESSING BUSINESS IMPROVEMENT DISTRICT EFFECTIVENESS

Our review of the four business improvement districts suggests that any assessment of success must include analysis of both *internal* and *external* organizational dynamics. The goals of business improvement districts are about improvement in the local business climate—especially through the delivery of additional services in the areas of sanitation, security, maintenance, and marketing. The ability to deliver these services effectively is contingent upon internal cohesion and consensus.

Internal Dynamics: Conflict and Consensus

Success or failure hinges on the degree to which there is unity within the organizational structure. Business improvement districts operate in the context of a diverse and changing group of property owners and merchants whose visions for downtown development differ as do their motives for situating their business in the district.

The "main street" business improvement districts (Fulton Mall and Jamaica Center) are made up of a more diverse and changing group of small and large merchants and property owners than the "corporate" BID (Metrotech). This diversity of owners and businesses fosters conflict over long-term and short-term development goals. Disagreements emerge due to (1) differences in vision between the "insiders"—made up of the long-standing property holders in the area, and "outsiders"—the newer property holders in the areas; and (2) differences in the economic perspectives of owners of small versus large amounts of property within the BID often create conflicts in goals. These differences inhibit consensus formation and diminish the potential for cooperation, thus reducing BID effectiveness.

Insiders versus Outsiders. The Fulton Mall BID provides a clear example of the problems of long-term versus short-term development visions within the organization. In 1992, Forest City Ratner Developers purchased Albee Square, an interior mall property on Fulton Street. Forest City Ratner, already a major player in the Metrotech BID because of their role as the developers of Metrotech, instantly became a significant entity in Fulton Mall as well by virtue of owning a major piece of retail property there. Forest City Ratner's vice president Paul Travis was also elected chairman of the Fulton Mall Improvement Association (FMIA). Conflict immediately surfaced among association members over short-term versus long-term visions. Travis advocated an increase in assessment levels to finance enhanced marketing and other economic development efforts so that large chain stores would locate in Fulton Mall. Within months, Travis was voted out of office by the district's long-established property owners. FMIA then took the opposite course and reduced BID assessment levels. The long-established property owners appeared unwilling to accept an increase in short-term cost for the sake of potentially greater long-term development. Nevertheless, Forest City pursued its long-term development strategy by upgrading its property holding on its own initiative and was able to attract a national retail chain store (Toys R Us) to their interior mall (which was renamed "The Gallery at Metrotech," despite its location in Fulton Mall). Meanwhile, the further development of Fulton Mall remains stymied because the property owners were unable to generate a plan to attract new retail tenants.

Forest City Ratner's vision was one of innovation and change (a long-term view), while a majority of the Fulton Mall property owners remained resistant to change and were unwilling to alter the status quo. The differences in vision within the Fulton Mall business improvement district continue. Jill Kelly, then executive director of the Fulton Mall Improvement Association, noted that:

The property owners here are niche retailers. Their attachment is to the dollar, to profits, not to the place. To understand the BID you need to understand the property owners and where they are coming from.

Competing Perspectives: Small versus Large Property Holders. Business improvement districts that are characterized by multiple property owners of different-sized parcels face additional internal conflicts due to their differing economic realities. Douglas Martin, writing in the New York Times (August 13, 1996), suggests that:

> it is a paradox of retailing that the biggest stores, the ones used as anchor stores to lure the smaller stores, pay less rent per square foot. The smaller stores pay considerably more, giving landlords their profits. But this works best when one developer owns all the space. Fulton Mall is owned in patchwork fashion by many parties, so it is harder to reach a consensus on what strategies the mall should adopt.

We can contrast this with the case at Metrotech. Here, a few owners of the major parcels of property in the BID dominate decision-making. Mike Weiss, current director of the Metrotech BID, states:

> Our success is also a function of the people . . . Chase, SIAC, and Forest City, they are the three that carry the BID the most.

Metrotech's ability to function as an economic development agent is significantly enhanced by the base of consensus among its major players. For example, Metrotech has recently selected the Lansco Company, a retail brokerage company, to market sites over ten thousand square feet in the area adjacent to the Commons to national retailers. Lansco will be targeting major retailers of books, computers, and clothing (Metrotech BID News, Summer 1996). To address problems of "attractiveness," Metrotech has also implemented a facade improvement program that will offer incentives to property owners who steam clean their buildings or remove unnecessary signage from their properties. Retail tenants may upgrade existing signage or replace solid roll-down gates with open mesh gates (Weiss interview).

All these programs are carried out at significant expense to the business improvement district, but the tenants of Metrotech look to the long term, not the short term. Charles Millard, former president of the New

York City Economic Development Corporation, stated that "Metrotech Center is one of the most successful economic development projects in the City of New York." (Metrotech BID News, Summer 1996)

External Impacts

Business Improvement Districts contribute to urban revitalization by creating stable, viable, and attractive economic environments. The true mark of BID success is in the popular perception of the area itself. In order to explore these qualitative aspects of BID success, particularly in relationship to the ability of business improvement districts to control the physical signs of decay, we carried out an "intercept survey" in which BID users (shoppers, employees, etc.) were asked a range of questions concerning their perceptions of the physical conditions of the area. In each of the four districts, respondents were asked:

1. How many years have you been coming to the area?

	Queens		Brooklyn	
	Jamaica %	*165th* %	*Fulton* %	*Metro.* %
Less than 5 years	33	48	46	43
More than 5 years	67	52	54	57

As the table above indicates, a majority of respondents in each district have been familiar with the area for many years, thus providing them with a long-term view, enabling them to gauge changes in the district over time.

BID users were asked to identify their primary reasons for coming to the area. The responses indicated that for 69 percent of the respondents in Fulton Mall and 51 percent of the respondents in 165th Street Mall, shopping was their main reason for coming to the area. In the case of Metrotech, 51 percent of respondents came to the area for work, although shopping was the second most common reason for coming to that area (38 percent of respondents). In the case of Jamaica Center, 53 percent of respondents came to the area for work and 40 percent came for shopping. This difference in usage patterns among our respondents is consistent with the differences mentioned previously with regard to the nature of activities and usages in these areas (retail versus commercial). In analyzing the responses to the above question, one significant difference between downtown Brooklyn and downtown Queens emerged: 50 percent of respondents in the combined Queens areas (Jamaica Center and 165th Street Mall) indicated that they live in the area. In contrast, less than 10 percent of the Brooklyn respondents (Fulton Mall and Metrotech) live in the area. Our findings confirm the long-held view of regional planners: Fulton Mall needs to be better integrated with its surrounding residential communities (Regional Plan Association, June 1983; Regional Plan Association, September 1996).

As mentioned above, the goals of business improvement districts include the creation of a cleaner and more comfortable environment. Respondents were asked several questions about their perception of physical appearances:

	Queens		Brooklyn	
	Jamaica *%*	*165th* *%*	*Fulton* *%*	*Metro.* *%*
2. Do you think the sidewalks and streets in the area are . . .				
Cleaner	58	28	55	85
The same	22	48	27	9
Dirtier	20	23	16	6
No answer	0	0	2	0
3. Has the appearance of the stores in the area . . .				
Improved	68	33	54	75
Stayed the same	22	47	32	23
Deteriorated	11	19	13	2
4. Has the appearance of the public spaces in the area . . .				
Improved	67	32	51	94
Stayed the same	20	47	37	6
Deteriorated	13	21	11	0

Although, in general, respondents in each district saw the BID as having positively contributed to the appearance of the area, there are clearly differences in popular perception as to how business improvement districts perform these services. An overwhelming majority of respondents rated Metrotech (the corporate BID) as being cleaner (85 percent), and having better storefronts (74 percent) and improved public spaces (94 percent). Fulton Mall and Jamaica Center (the main street

BIDs) also received high marks: between 51 and 68 percent of respondents, respectively, saw the areas as being cleaner and having improved storefronts and public spaces. The 165th Street Mall (the community BID) scored lower in each category. One possible explanation for these differences may be due to the availability of resources.

A second goal of business improvement districts is to create a safer environment. A safer environment results in more people shopping in the area, and it is more likely to attract other retailers.

	Queens		Brooklyn	
	Jamaica %	*165th* %	*Fulton* %	*Metro.* %
5. Do you think crime in the area has . . .				
Increased	21	29	16	13
Stayed the same	33	46	32	20
Decreased	44	24	51	54
No answer	2	0	0	0
6. Overall, how would you rate the general safety of the area?				
Good	49	39	35	60
Fair	31	35	52	36
Poor	20	26	13	4

Overall, respondents indicated that they felt that crime in the areas had decreased. According to official statistics, however, crime in New York City has gone down in recent years. We realized that responses to this question, therefore, might not reflect the work of the BID but of municipal services. In order to probe further, we also asked respondents to rate the general safety of the area. Once again, differences emerged in relations to BID type. For example, in Metrotech (the corporate BID), 54 percent of respondents felt crime in the area had decreased, and 60 percent rated the general safety of the area as good. The main street BIDs came next in terms of respondents' perceptions of the crime rate, but differences emerged with regard to perceptions of safety. While 51 percent of Fulton Mall respondents believed crime had decreased in the area, a majority (65 percent) rated security in the district as only fair to poor. The Regional Plan Association (1996) has argued that although crime is down, the perception of danger in the Brooklyn downtown area is a holdover from previous years. Jamaica Center scored higher on the safety question than did the Fulton Mall.

Forty-six percent of respondents in the community BID (165th Street Mall) felt that crime had stayed the same, and 29 percent actually felt crime had increased. These perceptions seem to be reflect the district's poor allocation of funds in its budget for safety and crime prevention.

The third aspect we explored concerned the users' perceptions of shopping in the area. One weakness in retailing areas is the failure to exploit its strength fully; that is, to serve all potential retail customers by providing a diverse shopping environment. Given the changing population bases in both downtowns, we felt it important to explore the degree to which business improvement districts are perceived to meet shoppers demands. Metrotech is not a retail center—thus, we do not include it in the following table.

	Queens		Brooklyn	
	Jamaica %	*165th* %	*Fulton* %	*Metro.* %
7. How would you rate shopping in the area?				
Good	60	58	45	
Fair	26	26	45	
Poor	14	16	10	

Janet Barkan, current director of the Jamaica Center BID, noted:

> I think the successes are quite visible here. A Conways came to Jamaica, this is their first Queens store, they saw that this was a commercial retail area with tremendous potential. Toys R Us, likewise, doesn't come into a community unless they think that they are going to do well.

The recent completion of Jamaica's "Farmers Market" (an international food court) serves as an added attraction to the area. Not surprisingly, 62 percent of the respondents rated Jamaica Center as a good area for eating out. Conversely, Fulton Mall's poor rating supports recent criticism that the area's retail mix needs upgrading to make it more attractive to a broader group of shoppers. As noted in a report by the Regional Plan Association (1996),

> [M]any sectors of the downtown Brooklyn community have expressed hope that this base of discount stores can be augmented by more name-brand stores featuring high-quality merchandise in more attractive,

service-oriented surroundings . . . A significant proportion of this potential consumer population remains untapped because of the current selection of stores.

The findings discussed above are consistent with differences we might have expected based on the BID typology proposed at the start of this chapter. Corporate business improvement districts, with larger budgets, greater expertise, and larger staffs, deliver a wider range of the most highly visible services (i.e., sanitation, security, and maintenance). Survey results on the "main street" and "community" business improvement districts are indicative of the lower levels of resources and capacity at their disposal. These results were strongly confirmed in the final survey question, in which we asked respondents to evaluate the overall impact of BID activities in their area.

	Queens		Brooklyn	
	Jamaica %	*165th* %	*Fulton* %	*Metro.* %
8. Has the impact of the BID been . . .				
Positive	68	41	80	100
No difference	27	55	20	0
Negative	5	4	0	0

While resources and expertise clearly affect the success or failure of business improvement districts as service providers, we found, in interviews, that other factors having to do with the internal dynamics of BID organizations also matter in the overall assessment of BID effectiveness.

Economic Development

Interview with business improvement district managers and city agency staff reiterated that one of the biggest problems that BID organizations must resolve is the difference in vision among property owners. Joyce Coward explains:

> In general, the large property owners are more forward-thinking. The smaller ones have terminal tunnel vision.

All of our data make clear that the "corporate" BID, Metrotech, for a variety of both internal and external reasons, was the most successful agent of economic development among the four business improvement districts. Internal cohesion, economic resources, and corporate managerial capacity combined to produce an effective organization engaged in development planning as well as day-to-day service delivery. As a creator of jobs and wealth, Metrotech has become a vital component of urban revitalization in downtown Brooklyn.

The main street business improvement districts at Fulton Mall and Jamaica Center can be viewed as limited successes in terms of economic development. These districts have had much greater challenges. Both districts have struggled to sustain physical redevelopment of their areas over time: redevelopment efforts were piecemeal and each project suffered delays and deterioration due to a lack of consensus. Yet despite all its problems, the Fulton Mall area still ranks sixth in sales amongst the nation's urban commercial streets (Martin 1993). Magic Johnson plans to make a major investment in Jamaica: to construct a sports and entertainment facility on the avenue. Thus, for the old main streets of urban downtowns, it appears that the mission of business improvement districts is to sustain existing investment until larger economic forces and broader changes in urban shopping patterns make them attractive sites for new investment and urban economic development.

Community business improvement districts remain the least studied of the three BID types. The current litigation in which the 165th Street Mall is involved hindered our case study by limiting our interviewing capacity. Our interviews with city officials and local development groups in Jamaica point out that community BIDs have been less successful in attracting and retaining business and in maintaining their physical infrastructure. Because of limited resources, community BIDs are vulnerable to breakdowns due to an inability to effectively deal with external and internal forces. Their limitations in resources, expertise, and consensus leads us to speculate that these types of BIDs can play only a limited role in promoting long-term economic redevelopment.

CONCLUSIONS AND RECOMMENDATIONS

Our study is confined to the role of business improvement districts and their potential as agents of urban economic revitalization. From our analysis we suggest five key elements for BID effectiveness: leadership, internal cohesion, agreement on mission, size, and financial resources. Under the proper organizational and environmental conditions, business improvement districts can be effective agents of economic development.

In view of decreasing federal resources for urban areas and the trends toward decentralization and privatization of service provision, business improvement districts can play an important role in the larger process of urban revitalization. The creation of a BID in and of itself is an action that mobilizes local property owners, businesses, local government, and community leaders to work together in the pursuit of community development. In the process of proposing a BID, the necessary outreach and ensuing dialogue engages the stakeholders in focusing on the development of a common agenda for the improvement of their area. The degree to which this process is effectively executed carries great portent for the future success of a BID organization. In this regard, the exercise of constructive leadership, the building of internal cohesion, and the agreement on mission are key ingredients for a healthy and enduring public-private partnership.

Business improvement districts can play two significant and distinct roles in urban revitalization processes. Initially, the role of the BID (corporate, main street, and community) tends to concentrate on the maintenance of physical infrastructure. When that physical redevelopment has been accomplished through the application of federal resources, as was the case with many large city development projects, business improvement districts become critical agents in preserving that investment.[7] The services that business improvement districts provide, such as supplementary sanitation and security, serve to maintain and extend the economic viability of business districts in central cities.

Corporate and main street business improvement districts, in particular, also serve as key incentives for attracting new businesses and preventing existing businesses from leaving the downtown. For BID members, participation can serve to broaden their perspective, promoting a sense of shared destiny rather than the narrow self-interest syndrome, to which small businesses are prone. In turn, the BID organization can direct its attention and resources to broader redevelopment efforts within its geographic area. Finally, the success of a business improvement district can stimulate attention to and spur development in surrounding areas.

In the context of current federal urban policy, our research on business improvement districts leads us to recommend the following:

- Federal programs for central city revitalization should include a requirement that local governments create mechanisms to maintain the investment of federal dollars in physical infrastructure development.

- Local governments should be required to exercise effective oversight and ongoing involvement in public—private partnerships.
- Local governments should be responsible for reporting to federal funding agencies on the creation, maintenance, and development of these mechanisms, and their effectiveness as agents of urban revitalization.
- Federal programs should include incentives (financial or otherwise) to reward local governments for successfully maintaining federally funded urban development projects.

As one such mechanism, business improvement districts have the potential to play a role in carrying out these recommendations. However, a complete appraisal of business improvement districts requires us to recognize both their strengths and weaknesses. Central among these is the matter of democratic accountability both within the BID organization and with respect to the larger community (i.e., local residents, other retail tenants, surrounding neighborhoods, and the city at large). Business improvement districts can become insular and isolated from the community that they are designed to serve. New York City, for example, mandates community outreach during the BID creation process only. As a result, according to the most recent city council report (November 12, 1997) on business improvement districts in New York:

> For many, Business improvement districts have inevitably become an unaccountable "micropolis" . . . where there is little or no disclosure regarding operations and services, and more importantly, the expenditure of assessments.[8]

A federal role is appropriate in promoting democratic accountability in business improvement districts as well as among other public—private partnership arrangements. The federal government should include a requirement that, as a condition of receiving financial assistance for urban revitalization, local governments institute mechanisms to promote the participation of stakeholders (property owners, business tenants, residents, local elected officials, and community organizations) in the ongoing governance of local development project areas.

Our research also revealed another question regarding intracity equality. The impact of business improvement districts in some, *but not all* areas of the city may result in tangible differences, or the perception thereof, in the delivery of basic services. It has been suggested that such a balkanization between BID and non—BID areas could weaken the city's overall vitality. Although not directly a matter of federal concern, we would like to suggest that there is a role for the federal government here. Federal government policies and programs should give consideration to the extent to which local governments implement federal assistance programs for urban revitalization so as to achieve broader equity within the central city as a whole.

Addressing these broader democratic issues in the construction of a comprehensive framework for the evaluation of business improvement districts or other public-private partnership mechanisms is a task that compels future analyses.

NOTES

[1]In this report we use the term "BID" to refer to both BIDs and SADs as a convenience for the reader The primary difference between these districts is rooted in their legislative origins. In practice, in New York City, these districts operate in similar fashion to each other. For a fuller discussion of this distinction see this chapter.

[2]A second survey, directed to the property owners in the four BID areas under study, was also undertaken, to generate additional measures to more fully assess the successes and failures of business improvement districts as agents of economic development. A questionnaire was mailed to more than three hundred owners of record for all the blocks and lots within the relevant geographic areas. Owners were identified with the assistance of the New York City Department of Finance. The response rate was so poor that it was not possible to undertake a worthwhile analysis of this data. The New York City Council, in its ongoing effort to conduct oversight of business improvement districts, has encountered similar difficulties (see New York City Council Report, November 12, 1997, p. 20).

[3]In our interviews we explore this question in depth. In our previous study, we found that the success of CDBG/UDAG/UMTA-funded projects rested to a large degree upon strong partnerships; thus, one must consider the degree to which such partnerships impact upon the success or failure of business improvement districts as sustainers of these same projects.

[4]This negative approval practice has raised questions about the democracy and accountability of business improvement districts. We will consider the impact of this upon BID success and failure, but it is not our intention in the current study to focus on issues of democracy broadly.

[5]The data recorded in Figure 4–1, was current as of 1995, at which time thirty business improvement districts had been formally established. Since that

time nine additional business improvement districts were approved, bringing the total number of business improvement districts in New York City to thirty-nine.

[6]Like the District Management Associations created to administer business improvement districts, the Fulton Mall Improvement Association (FMIA) is a nonprofit organization whose board includes city government representatives and local private sector members.

[7]In the four BID case studies explored in this research, significant federal funding had been provided in the form of Urban Development Action Grants, Community Development Block Grants, and Urban Mass Transit Administration funds.

We would like to express our appreciation to Professor Andrew Parker and his students in the School of Public Affairs, Baruch College, CUNY, for their assistance in conducting the BID User Survey for this project. Their efforts were essential in implementing this aspect of our research.

REFERENCES

An Engine for Economic Development Downtown. (1994, May 29.) *New York Times.*

"A Report on Progress and Growth. Brooklyn's Fulton Mall." A Report Produced by the Fulton Mall Improvement Association (Winter 1979).

Beam, John M. "New York City's Business Improvement Districts: An Evaluation." A report from the New York City Economic Policy and Marketing Group, Working Paper Number 94–3 (May 1995).

Bennett, Robert, ed. *Decentralizing Local Governments and Markets.* Oxford, UK: Clarendon Press, 1994.

Business Improvement Districts Face Resistance to Explosive Growth. (1995, June 12.) *Crains New York Business.*

Business improvement districts in for Fulton Mall Phase II. *Fulton Mall News*, Vol. 6, No. 9 (1982, August 27).

City Council Orders Review of 33 Business Improvement Districts. (1995, April 19.) *New York Times.*

City of New York, Department of City Planning. "An Overview of Business Improvement Districts in New York City and Other Selected Metropolitan Areas." A report prepared for the New York City Planning Commission's Hearing on Business Improvement Districts (Autumn 1995).

Cott, Sue. "Bridging the Gap: Business Improvement Districts." *WCBS–TV Editorial.* (1982, April.)

Council of the City of New York. "Cities Within Cities: Business Improvement Districts and the Emergence of the Micropolis." A report prepared for the Finance Committee (November 8, 1995).

Council of the City of New York, "Managing the Micropolis: Proposals to Strengthen BID Performance and Accountability." (November 12, 1997).

Dommel, Paul R. et al. *Decentralizing Urban Policy.* Washington, DC: The Brookings Institution, 1982.

Downtown Boomtown. *Fulton Mall News*, Vol. 6, No. 2 (1982, February 9).

Downtown Brooklyn Pushes for Brighter Future. *The Phoenix* (1983, July 21).

Economic Development Staff of the New York City Partnership and New York City Chamber of Commerce and Industry, "A Strategy to Support Business Improvement Districts: Facing the Emerging Issues." A Report Prepared for the Business Improvement District Task Force (April 1995).

Fainstein, Susan S. "The Changing World Economy and Urban Restructuring." In *Leadership and Urban Regeneration*, Dennis Judd and Michael Parkinson (eds.) Thousand Oaks, CA: Sage, 1990.

Fulton Mall Improvement Association, "Annual Report" (1995, May 2).

Fulton Mall Improvement Association, "A Report on Progress and Growth." (Winter 1979).

Fulton Mall Improvement Association Hires Private Security Force. *Fulton Mall News*, Vol. 4, No. 12 (1980, July 18).

Houstoun, Lawrence O. Jr. Betting on Business Improvement Districts. In *Urban Land* (Urban Land Institute, Washington, DC: 1994).

Houstoun, Lawrence O. Jr. "Six Tests for State Enabling Legislation." In *City Center Report* (Washington, DC: International Downtown Associations). (April 1992).

Imbruscio, David L. "Economic Development." In *Handbook of Research on Urban Politics and Policy*, R. Vogel (ed.). Westport, CT: Greenwood Press, 1997.

Is B.I.D. Plan One Too Many? (1995, Sept. 3). *New York Times.*

Jacobs, S. and K. Saffro, "Betting on Business Improvement Districts." In *Metropolitics*, Barnard–Columbia Center for Urban Policy (May 1996).

Jamaica: Security and Sanitation Are Priorities in a New Business District. (1996, February 11). *New York Times.*

Judd, Dennis and Todd Swanstrom. *City Politics: Private Power & Public Policy.* New York: HarperCollins, 1994.

Kantor, Paul. *The Dependent City.* Reading, MA: Scott, Foresman, 1988.

KRC Research and Consulting, "Street-Intercept Survey: Perceptions of Business Improvement Districts and Conditions in the Grand Central, Bryant Park and 34th Street Areas." Research Report Prepared for the Grand Central Partnership (October 1994).

Logan, John R. and Todd Swanstrom (eds.). *Beyond the City Limits.* Philadelphia, PA: Temple University Press, 1990.

MacDonald, Heather. "BIDs Really Work." *City Journal.* New York: The Manhatten Institute (Spring 1996).

Martin, Douglas, "Thriving Mall Seeks Image to Match." (August 16, 1993) *New York Times.*

Metrotech BID News. Vol. 4, No. 3 (Spring 1996).

Metrotech BID News. Vol. 4, No. 4 (Summer 1996).

More Rules for Business Districts? (April 26, 1993). *Daily News.*

New York City Administrative Code, 25–401 through 25–417, Title 25, Chapter 4. "City Business Improvement Districts."

New York City Department of Business Services. "Business Improvement Districts in Planning" (June 1996).

New York City Department of Business Services. "Commercial Revitalization Program: An Overview" (May 1996).

New York City Department of Business Services. "Establishing and Operating a Business Improvement District: A Step by Step Guide" (February 1996).

New York City Department of Business Services. "New York City Business Improvement Districts" (August 1995).

New York City Department of Business Services. "Starting and Managing Business Improvement Districts" (July 1995).

New York City Department of City Planning. "An Overview of Business Improvement Districts in New York City and Other Selected Metropolitan Areas" (February, 1996).

New York City General Municipal Law, Article 19–a, Sections 980 through 980–p. "Business Improvement Districts."

Pecorella, R. "Fiscal Crises and Regime Change: A Contextual Approach." In *The Politics of Urban Development,* Clarence Stone and Heywood Sanders (eds.). Lawrence, KA: University of Kansas Press, 1987.

Peterson, Paul. *City Limits.* Chicago: University of Chicago, 1981.

Polytechnic, City Spur 171M complex (1982, April 16). *Daily News.*

Regional Plan Association, "Downtown Brooklyn: A Plan for Progress." (September 1996).

Regional Plan Association, "Downtown Brooklyn: A Report." *Regional Plan News*, Number 114 (June 1983).

Rogowsky, Edward T., Ronald Berkman, et al. "New York City's Outer Borough Development Strategy." In *Urban Revitalization Policies and Programs,* Fritz Wagner, Timothy Joder, and Anthony Mumphrey Jr., (eds.). Thousand Oaks, CA: Sage Publications, 1995.

Ross, Bernard H. and Myron A. Levine. *Urban Politics: Power in Metropolitan America*, 5th ed. Itasca, IL: F. E. Peacock, 1996.

Squires, Gregory D. "Partnership and the Pursuit of the Private City." In *Urban Life in Transition*, M. Gottdiener and Chris Pickvance. Thousand Oaks, CA: Sage, 1991.

Stone, Clarence, "The Study of the Politics of Urban Development." In *The Politics of Urban Development*, Clarence Stone and Heywood Sanders (eds.). Lawrence, KA: University of Kansas, 1987.

Street Fight: Unions Versus B.I.D.'s (1996, March 24). *New York Times*.

Time Square on the Mend. (1995. October 8). *Atlanta Journal Constitution*.

Thirty—six Businesses Unite to Create New 180th St. Business Improvement District. *Gateway Jamaica Newsletter*, Vol. 1, No. 1 (1996).

Why Business Improvement Districts Work (1996, July). *Civic Bulletin*.

Williams, Peter and Neil Smith. "From 'Renaissance' to Restructuring: The Dynamics of Contemporary Urban Development." In *Enduring Tensions in Urban Politics*, Dennis Judd and Paul Kantor (eds.). Indianapolis: Macmillan, 1992.

INTERVIEW LIST

Outerborough BID Administrators, Property Owners, and Directors

Jill Kelly, executive director, FMIA (current)

Mike Strasser, Fulton Mall (former director)

Mike Weiss, Metrotech (current director)

Ken Adams, Metrotech (former director)

Janet Barkan, Jamaica Center (current director)

Jerry Gertz, 165th St./Jamaica Center, property owner (former president)

Bob Ohleriking, Fulton Mall (former Director), and Downtown Brooklyn Development Association (former director)

Tessie Williams, district manager, Community Board 2, Brooklyn

Carlisle Towery, executive director of Greater Jamaica Development Corporation (GJDC)

Helen Levine, executive vice president, GJDC

Daniel Kulka, property owner, Jamaica

Paul Travis, Forest City Ratner Developers

Surveys have been sent to all property owners in the 4 BID areas.

Manhattan BID Directors

Carl Weisbrod, director, Downtown Alliance

Tom Cusik, director, 5th Avenue BID and founder, NYC BID Managers Association

Rob Walsh, director, 14th Street/Union Square BID
Gretchen Dykstra, director, 42nd Street BID

Government Agencies

Barbara Wolff, assistant commissioner, Department of Business Services (DBS)
Joyce Coward, director, Technical Assistance Programs, DBS
Leon Fonfa, senior BID manager, DBS
Eddy Evy, senior BID manager, DBS
Nicholas Pappas, manager, Economic Development Zones, DBS
Stephen Small Warner, senior development manager, DBS
Bill Chong, staff, U.S. Deptartment of Housing and Urban Development (HUD),
    NYC Regional Office
Jack Johnson, staff, HUD, Regional Office
David Burns, staff, HUD, Regional Office
Anthony Magri, staff, HUD, Regional Office
Paul Bonnett, staff, HUD, Regional Office
Eric Kober, director of housing economic and infrastructure planning, Depart-
    ment of City Planning
Barry Dinerstein, deputy director of housing economic and infrastructure plan-
    ning, Department of City Planning
Bill Donohue, staff, Department of City Planning
Mitchel Korby, director, Brooklyn office, Department of City Planning

Others

David Gallagher, Coalition for Neighborhood Economic Development
Rita Schwartz, Partnership for the Homeless
Liz Abzug, economic development consultant

CHAPTER 5

Sports Stadia: A Strategy for Downtown Redevelopment

ARTHUR C. NELSON

WHITHER STADIA?

Many business and political leaders believe that major league sports facilities are a critical element of a city's or a metropolitan area's economic and social, if not political, vitality. From the beginning of modern major league sports more than one hundred years ago, many cities considered themselves inferior to those that boasted major league teams. The past twenty years have seen the culture of major league sports turn against the very cities that sowed the seeds to make major league sports what it is today. Nowadays, major league teams hold their cities hostage for multiple hundreds of millions of dollars in facilities and concessions. The Atlanta Braves Baseball Club, for example, grew by more than fifty million dollars in market value by inheriting use of the 1996 Olympic Stadium for only the cost of conversion.

During the past twenty years, cities have also built facilities to attract conventions and trade shows, theater productions, and shoppers. These and related efforts are attempts by cities either to revitalize slumping economies or maintain their regional prominence, or both. In the scheme of things, sport stadia are now only one part of any city's economic development strategy. They may also be among the most debatable of economic development investments.

The debate surrounding the efficacy of sports stadia seems especially rancorous. On one side are political pragmatists who offer no apologies for committing hundreds of millions of dollars in public funds, follow through with a commitment by a team to locate or relocate to the city, or speculate on the ability to attract a major league team with no particular concern about economic development return. It is as though what matters most is the city's association with a major league team, not whether the public investment pays off. On the other side of the debate are those policy analysts and some politicians who openly question the investment value of such public funds. A third camp offers that under certain conditions sports stadia are important economic development components of central cities.

This research addresses the economic development debate from a different albeit important angle. At least part of the debate surrounding the wisdom of public investment in major sports stadia is misplaced. The question evaluated here is not whether public investment *per se* is worthwhile from an economic development perspective, but *where* that investment should be directed once the decision has been made to build. From a metropolitan or regional economic development perspective, should a stadium be built in the central business district (CBD), the edge of the CBD, elsewhere in the central city, or in the suburbs? The hypothesis tested here is rather straightforward: Centrally located stadia will generate greater economic activity than remote stadia.

This chapter is composed of four sections. The first reviews the relevant literature. The second builds a theory on the association between the location and urban design of a sports stadium and metropolitan economic activity. The third evaluates the theory using empirical evidence. The last section offers conclusions and policy implications.

But first a word on nomenclature. Although the term "professional sports stadia" is applied to major league sports in this study, the concept and the findings of this work are easily applied to all professional sports venues, whether major or minor league, or emerging (such as professional women's basketball, indoor football, and soccer).

LITERATURE REVIEW

Professional sports teams and the stadia in which they play are viewed by many as prerequisites for being considered "world class" or at least "major league" (Baade and Dye 1990). In recent years, owners of professional sports teams have often been able to receive local government subsidies ranging into eight digits to stay in their hometowns or relocate (Okner 1974; Quirk 1987; Baade and Dye 1988; Baim 1990). While this may be considered a high price to pay for major league status, some argue that the direct and indirect economic benefits offset public subsidies (Northeastern Illinois Planning Commission 1986; Norton 1993). Typical of studies alleging metropolitanwide benefits of professional teams is one reported by Deloitte and Touche (1993) that projected an annual economic output from a new stadium in Phoenix to be $162 million for the city and $230 million for the state of Arizona. Follow-up studies on actual impact are not common although a study of the New Orleans Superdome showed that it had a strong, positive impact on Louisiana's economy (Nebel 1986). Baade (1996) concludes that such prospective and retrospective studies exaggerate the importance of sports stadia since they apply only input-output coefficients and do not look at actual changes in jobs or income, much less the opportunity costs, when considering alternative investments.

A growing literature not only fails to associate professional teams and their stadia with improving metropolitan economic conditions (Baade and Dye 1988; Baade and Dye 1990; Rosentraub, Swindell, Przybylski, and Mullins 1994; Baade 1994; Quirk 1987; Quirk and Fort 1992; Euchner 1993; Greco 1994), but suggest that public subsidies of stadia may actually send the economy backward because of opportunity costs (Baim 1990; 1992).

There is also debate regarding whether local investment in stadia as a means by which to revitalize certain areas is effective. In their assessment of the impact of the Hoosier Dome and Market Square Arena on downtown and nearby neighborhood economic activity, Rosentraub, Swindell, Przybyski, and Mullins (1994) observe:

> While there were important achievements which should be attributed to Indianpolis's sports strategy, on balance it seems fair to conclude there were no significant or substantial shifts in economic development. (p. 236)

In perhaps the most rigorous study reported to date on the association between professional sports stadia and metropolitan economic activity, Baade (1996) concluded that the evidence was ambiguous at best. In his evaluation of economic effects observed in ten cities, Baade found that major league stadia had positive and mostly significant influences[a] in Cincinnati, Kansas City, Indianapolis, Minneapolis, Pittsburgh, and Seattle, and negative influences in Baltimore, Denver, Detroit, New Orleans, Oakland, San Diego, San Francisco, and Washington, D.C. Baade thus found no conclusive pattern to the effect of sports stadia on the economies of these selected metropolitan areas.

Baade's (1996) work hints that there is something else going on that helps explain in which cities sports stadia have positive influences and in which they have negative or ambiguous impacts. In those cities where economic impacts are positive, stadia are located at or very close to downtown. These cities include Indianapolis, Cincinnati, and Pittsburgh. In three other cities with positive signs—Kansas City, Minneapolis, and Seattle—stadia are designed to connect pedestrians to downtowns or nearby activity centers through dedicated pedestrian ways or the linkage of retail outlets from downtown to those stadia. In contrast, in those cities where negative associations were found, stadia are located far away from downtowns or nearby activity centers. They include Denver,[b] Detroit, Oakland, San Diego, San Francisco, and Washington, D.C.

It is the very ambiguity presented in Baade's work that stimulates consideration that what matters most about professional sports stadia is not the question of whether they should be built, but rather if they are to be built, where they should be located. The evidence suggested but not explored by the literature is that from the perspective of a metropolitan economy there may be important associations between professional sports stadia location and metropolitan economic development (and by extension with central city vitality). Why is this?

Attending professional sporting events is a socializing experience. Grecian and Roman societies built coliseums in the centers of cities, providing citizens with the most accessible location in which to enjoy sporting events (Peterson 1996). Major theaters, symphonies, museums, and the like find central locations crucial to their survival. Once at these recreational venues, people will take advantage of other things near them, such as stores, restaurants, and other points of interest. By locating professional sports stadia downtown, downtown merchants benefit from pre- and postgame celebration (or commiseration). Once downtown because of the event, fans are more likely there than elsewhere to patronize stores, spend the evening in hotels, and visit other attractions such as museums and art galleries.

The farther professional sports venues are from the center of things, the less likely people are to patronize merchants before or after events if for no other reason than there are few or no merchants to patronize. To capture spectators' dollars, especially where stadia are located away from downtowns or other activity centers, stadia management offer expanded concessions. Thus, sushi is offered in San Diego's Jack Murphy Stadium, which is located several miles from downtown at the intersection of two interstate highways. But expanded concession offerings may be poor substitutes, especially for pre- and postgame activities. Indeed, despite observations by Rosentraub et al. that the Hoosier Dome and Market Square Arena in downtown Indianapolis do much to internalize spectator spending during events, this researcher has found it difficult to find a restaurant available for pre- and postevent meals without reservations. There is little problem during nonevent days, however.

Theory and Model

The theory posited here is that *the closer a professional sports stadium is to the center of the central business district, the greater the economic benefits to the metropolitan area.* The theory builds particularly on work done by Baade and Dye (1990) and Baade (1994, 1996), who found generally that sports stadia and by implication professional sports teams playing in them have no clearly positive or statistically significant effect on metropolitan income. They reason that within metropolitan areas the presence of professional sports opportunities merely displaces spending from other leisure pursuits; professional sports are thus a kind of zero-sum game.

But there are reasons why stadia may generate new economic activity in the metropolitan-area. If sports spending is merely a substitute for leisure among metropolitan-area residents, it may be better to consider the possibility that professional sports import resources by exporting professional sports attendance into the region outside the metropolitan area. This can happen if nonmetropolitan-area residents attend games (sports service exportation) or if metropolitan-area residents who would have spent some leisure resources away from home instead stay home to attend games (import substitution).

Following Baade (1996), a model is developed here to measure the extent to which professional stadia are attractors of resources from outside the metropolitan area, thereby improving its balance of trade position with the outside world. Two measures are considered. First, if a professional sports stadium and the teams playing therein attract resources from outside the region, the metropolitan area's share of regional income will rise after considering all other factors. Second, it should follow that the metropolitan area's share of recreation income should also rise after considering other factors. Expanding from Baade's original formulation, the model includes stadia location and regional control factors.

(1) *MSA SHARE OF STATE or REGION INCOME =*
     f{ECONOMIC FACTORS, TIME, REGION, SPORTS STADIA
     LOCATION}

In this formulation, the dependent variables are:
$(MSA–PERSONAL–INCOME_{i,t}$ / $REGION–PERSONAL–INCOME_{j,t})$ is
metropolitan area i's share of region j's aggregate personal income at
time t, which hereinafter is known as *MSA–SHARE–(STATE or RE-
GION)–INCOME*, and $(MSA–RECREATION–INCOME_{i,t}$ / *REGION–
RECREATION–INCOME$_{j,t}$*) is metropolitan area i's share of region j's
personal income from SIC Code 79 (the amusement and recreation industry) at time t, which hereinafter is known as *MSA–SHARE–(STATE or
REGION)–REC.–INCOME*, and the independent variables are:

Economic Factors

$(MSA–PER–CAPITA–INCOME_{i,t}$ / $REGION–PER–CAPITA–$
$INCOME_{j,t})$ is the ratio of metropolitan area i's real personal per
capita income to the real personal per capita income of region j, hereinafter known as *MSA–(STATE or REGION)–INCOME–RATIO*;
$(MSA–DURABLE–INCOME_{i,t}$ / $REGION–DURABLE–INCOME_{j,t})$
is the ratio of metropolitan area i's real personal per capita income
from durable goods manufacturing to the real personal per capita income of region j in durable goods manufacturing, hereinafter known
as *MSA–SHARE–(STATE or REGION)–MANUF.INCOME*; *MSA–
POPULATION–CHANGE*$_{i,t}$ is the ratio of metropolitan area i's population in year t to year $t–1$;

Time

$YEAR_i$ is the year of observation of metropolitan area i.

Region

$RUSTBELT_i$ is a binary (dummy) control for metropolitan areas located in the New England and Middle Atlantic census divisions, a
region of stagnant growth during the study period which is used as
the referent against which all other regions are compared;

$MISSISSIPPI–VALLEY_i$ is a binary (dummy) control for metropolitan areas located along and west of the Mississippi River, a region
historically connected by the river and which tends to grow or decline together (New Orleans and St. Louis);

$SOUTHEAST_i$ is a binary (dummy) control for metropolitan areas in the Southeast and East South Central census divisions, a region of economic ascendancy east of the Mississippi River;

$SOUTHWEST\text{–}MOUNTAIN_i$ is a binary (dummy) control for metropolitan areas in the West North Central, Mountain, and Southwest census divisions, a region within which metropolitan areas having professional sports teams essentially comprise the sunbelt west of the Mississippi Valley;

$PACIFIC_i$ is a binary (dummy) control for metropolitan areas in the Pacific census division; and

Sports Stadia Location

$TEAMS\text{–}CBD_{i,t}$ is the number of professional sports teams playing in the central business district of metropolitan area i in year;

$TEAMS\text{–}CBD\text{–}EDGE_{i,t}$ is the number of professional sports teams playing at the edge of the central business district of metropolitan area i in year t (adjacent to the CBD but separated by water, major highways, railroads, or other major barriers to pedestrian access to the CBD);

$TEAMS\text{–}OTHER\text{–}CENTRAL\text{–}CITY_{i,t}$ is the number of professional sports teams otherwise playing in the central city of metropolitan area i in year t

$TEAMS\text{–}SUBURB_{i,t}$ is the number of professional sports teams playing outside the central city of metropolitan area i in year $t;$ e_t is the stochastic disturbance.

What is the region? There are three options. Baade (1996) defined the region as the state. This seems reasonable, as fans align themselves with teams mostly within state boundaries. The Minnesota Twins baseball team probably attracts fewer patrons from Wisconsin because Wisconsin fans probably align themselves more with the Milwaukee Brewers baseball team. The disadvantage in using states as the region is that cities on borders between two states attract from both states, and if only the home state is evaluated, economic effects may be underestimated.

It may be better to define each metropolitan region more carefully. Perhaps, for example, the trade area of the city's major newspaper could proxy for the true region of a metropolitan area. The alternative would be the Bureau of Economic Analysis's (BEA) 238 economic areas (Bureau of Economic Analysis 1977), which are based in part on the circulation of major papers. This, too, may underestimate the region. For example, the Atlanta Braves baseball team will attract fans from no fewer than five BEA economic areas in two states (Georgia and Tennessee), and there is some evidence that the Kansas City football and baseball teams attract fans from no fewer than six states. Finally, if one considers that professional sports sometimes competes for fans from overlapping market areas, such as the Philadelphia and Pittsburgh professional teams, both of which extend into several nearby states, the problem of defining the region for any given sports franchise is difficult. Perhaps the Census Bureau's nine census regions are a reasonable albeit crude definition of the word "region."

At some level, one may consider the nation as the region of at least some teams. The Dallas Cowboy football franchise and the Atlanta Braves baseball franchise claim to be "America's team" for their respective sports. Most of the New York Yankees baseball franchise fans may be found outside New York City, and even outside its metropolitan area. On the other hand, few Yankees fans living outside the Boston–Washington conurbation will make the trek to Yankee Stadium, so economic "attraction" is limited to an area much smaller than the nation.

The two "regions" used in this analysis are defined as the state (following Baade) and the nine census regions. While still crude in both respects, analysis should reveal trends that are generalizable for public policy purposes.

Economic data for personal income, durable goods personal income, and recreation and amusement personal income (SIC 79) come from the Bureau of Economic Analysis's Regional Economic Information System, available online through the University of Virginia. Those data are organized by county, state, and metropolitan area for each of the years 1969 through 1994. Metropolitan area data are based on 1990 Metropolitan Statistical Area (MSA) definitions of the Census Bureau. Figures are adjusted to 1994 dollars based on the consumer price index for the nation, as reported in the *Statistical Abstract of the United States 1996*.

Information on the location of professional sports stadia and the teams that played in them during the study period is pieced together from a variety of sources, mostly from *USA Today*'s *The Complete Four Sports Stadium Guide* (1996), the *Information Please Sports Almanac* (1996), and various city maps.

Because the research question focuses on whether different loca-

tions of professional sports stadia affect metropolitan economies differ-
ently, the analysis is limited to those MSAs that had at least one professional sports team during the study period.[c] (Table 5–1 reports all 44
metropolitan areas with sports teams during the study period.)

Baade's recent work (1996) analyzed two sets of data. The first was
a set of ten MSAs that have major league stadia and the second was a
larger set of forty-eight MSAs, only about a third of which have stadia.
This analysis is applied to those forty-four MSAs which have or have
had professional sports teams, and for which complete data are available.[d] There are three reasons for this. First, with up to four location options (CBD, edge, other central city, and suburb) and four sports options
(baseball, basketball, football, and hockey), there are insufficient degrees
of freedom in which to evaluate the effects of stadia location on individual MSAs. Second and more to the point, differences in location effects
are tested best in cross-sectional analysis that compensates for MSA-
specific influences such as the effect of prolonged periods of winning or
loosing seasons on sports-related economic activity. Third, by restricting
the analysis only to those MSAs with professional sports stadia and
teams, the problem of simultaneity is reduced if not eliminated.

Like Baade's study, (1996) this research uses a variable for durable
goods manufacturing. Baade (1996) used the ratio of the number of
hours worked per week in the durable goods sector in the metropolitan
area to the number worked in the state as an indicator of leisure time (the
lower the ratio, the higher the leisure time). It is probably a better indicator of manufacturing employment than of leisure; after all, unemployed
workers who have unlimited hours of leisure are not likely to be able to
afford to attend many professional sporting events. But because durable
goods jobs are generally higher paid than jobs in most other sectors (at
least at the two-digit SIC level), it may indicate the wealth of the metropolitan area relative to other areas, and indicate the strength of the metropolitan area's export base relative to other areas. Because the share of the
state's durable goods personal income attributable to a metropolitan area,
helps explain the variation in the share of total state income attributable
to a metropolitan area, and so that variable is use.

Lastly, whereas Baade and Dye (1990) and Baade (1996) include
an MSA population variable in their previous work, this researcher
found *MSA–SHARE–(STATE or REGION)–INCOME* and *MSA– SHARE–
(STATE or REGION)–REC.–INCOME* to be collinear with MSA population, which is not surprising. Because the dependent variables already
account for relative contributions of MSA size to the region, using a pop-

Table 5–1
Metropolitan Areas with Professional Sports Franchises,
1969–1994

MSA	Baseball	Football	Basketball	Hockey
Anaheim (Orange County)	X			X
Atlanta	X	X	X	X
Baltimore	X	X	X	
Boston/Foxboro	X	X	X	2X
Buffalo		X		X
Charlotte			X	
Chicago	2X	X	X	X
Cincinnati	X	X		
Cleveland	X	X	X	
Dallas/Irving		X	X	X
Denver	X	X	X	X
Detroit/Pontiac/Auburn Hills	X	X	X	X
Fort Worth/Arlington	X			
Northeast New Jersey	X	2X	X	X
Green Bay		X		
Hartford				X
Houston	X	X	X	
Indianapolis		X	X	
Kansas City	X	X	X	
Los Angeles	X	X		
Miami	X	X	X	
Milwaukee	X		X	
Minneapolis-St. Paul	X	X	X	X
New Haven				X
New Orleans		X	X	
New York	X	X	X	X
Oakland	X	X	X	
Omaha				X

Orlando		X	
Philadelphia	X	X	X	X
Phoenix		X	X	
Pittsburgh	X	X		X
Portland			X	
Sacramento			X	
Salt Lake City			X	
San Antonio			X	
San Diego	X	X	X	
San Francisco	X	X	X	X
San Jose				X
Seattle	X	X	X	
Springfield, MA				X
St. Louis	X	X		X
Tampa Bay		X		
Washington, DC/Landover, MD	X	X	X	X

ulation variable on the right-hand side seems inappropriate. However, population change is relevant because it accounts for year-to-year effects on the MSA's share of state income caused by events specific to the MSA (such as gaining or loosing a major manufacturing firm).

Evaluation Strategy

Three evaluations are undertaken, for three different reasons. In order to evaluate differences in metropolitan-area economies with respect to the number of professional sports teams and where they play within the MSA, cross-section analysis is most appropriate. This can be done for any given year but the number of MSAs having professional sports teams during any given year will be less than forty, so there would be insufficient degrees of freedom in which to test for effects. Multiple years generates more observations. The results will indicate whether and the extent to which professional teams playing in different parts of MSAs influence the MSA economy. The general model used here is:

(MSA–SHARE–(STATE or REGION)–INCOME) and
(MSA–SHARE–(STATE or REGION)–REC.–INCOME) =
    f{MSA–RATIO–(STATE or REGION)–INCOME, MSA–SHARE–
    (STATE or REGION)–MANUF.–INCOME, MSA–POPULATION–
    CHANGE, YEAR, RUSTBELT, MISSISSIPPI–VALLEY,
    SOUTHEAST, SOUTHWEST–MOUNTAIN, PACIFIC, TEAMS–
    CBD, TEAMS–CBD–EDGE, TEAMS–OTHER–CENTRAL–CITY,
    TEAMS–SUBURB}.

For regressions defining the region as the census region, the regional controls are removed to avoid overspecification. Results of this analysis are reported in Table 5–2.

Cross-section analysis does not answer the chicken-or-the-egg question: Do professional teams contribute to the local economy or are they merely attracted to it, responding only to a demand for leisure? Two-stage least squares analysis helps answer this question. The first stage equation is the cross-section specification except that *TEAMS–CBD* and *TEAMS–CBD–EDGE* are grouped into *TEAMS–DOWNTOWN* because the second stage equation is:

TEAMS–CBD =
    f{MSA–SHARE–REGION–INCOME, MSA–RATIO–REGION–
    CAPITA–INCOME, MSA–SHARE–MANUF.–INCOME, MSA–
    POPULATION–CHANGE, YEAR, RUSTBELT, MISSISSIPPI–
    VALLEY, SOUTHEAST, SOUTHWEST–MOUNTAIN, PACIFIC}.

An ambiguous relationship between *TEAMS-CBD* and *MSA– SHARE–REGION–INCOME* would suggest that professional sports teams playing in the CBD indeed contribute to the local economy without respect to the local economy's size or growth dynamics. A positive association would suggest interaction between the two, which is to be expected. The regional controls are removed for regressions defining the region as the census region to avoid overspecification. Results of this analysis are reported in Table 5–3.

There is the concern about how MSAs are defined spatially—not that this research attempts to second-guess the Bureau of the Census. Moreover, there may be problems of serial (time-series) correlation for individual cities. Both may be addressed through Cochrane-Orcutt evaluation using the following specification:

(MSA–SHARE–REGION–INCOME) =
f{MSA–RATIO–REGION–INCOME, MSA–SHARE–REGION–
MANUF.–INCOME, MSA–POPULATION–CHANGE, YEAR,
TEAMS–CBD, TEAMS–CBD–EDGE, TEAMS–OTHER–
CENTRAL–CITY, TEAMS–SUBURB}.

If an MSA is small relative to the market for professional sports, the introduction of professional sports should result in an increase in the MSA's share of regional income for the simple reason that a higher percentage of fans come from outside the region. Moreover, as postulated herein, MSAs where teams play in central locations will benefit more relative to those MSAs where teams play in the suburbs.

But if an MSA is large either in economic volume or in territory, it is more likely to attract only those fans (and their dollars) that would have be consumed on leisure in the MSA anyway. In these situations, no effect is anticipated.

The Cochrane-Orcutt analysis can only be applied to those MSAs that had professional sports over several years during the study period (four years is the minimum imposed), and which involved teams playing in several locations, or at least one team moving from one location to another. Twenty-five MSAs met those filtering criteria.

Results and Interpretations

Results and interpretations of cross-section, two-stage least squares, and Cochrane-Orcutt evaluations are presented in this section. Conclusions and policy implications follow.

Cross-Section Evaluation Table 5–2 presents the results of the four cross-section regression equations. All equations possessed reasonably good coefficients of determination and F-ratios. A correlation matrix found no problematic colinearity between variables.[e] Systematic patterns of bias were not evident in the casewise plot of standardized residuals against the dependent variable, although some patterns for individual MSAs are suspected; but these suspicions are addressed in the Cochrane-Orcutt time-series analyses of individual MSAs reported later. Coefficients had reasonable magnitudes, and where directions of association were predicted the signs were mostly as expected or explainable (regional control variables have no predictable directions of association *per se*).

Table 5–2
Cross-Section Evaluation of Professional Team Locations and Metropolitan Share of Region Economic Activities

Variable and Statistic	Dependent Variable			
	MSA-SHARE-STATE-INCOME	MSA-SHARE-STATE–REC-INCOME	MSA-SHARE-REGIONAL-INCOME	MSA-SHARE-REGIONAL-REC-INCOME
MSA-RATIO-PER-CAPITA-INCOME	28.737798 (3.758921)*	38.215694 (4.248187)*	2.111923 (1.344783)	13.291350 (1.653068)*
MSA-SHARE-MANUF-INCOME	.946903 (.022155)*	.868213 (.025093)*	.970480 (.025961)*	1.006471 (.032157)*
MSA-POP-CHANGE	-.217684 (.351158)	1.352069 (.419322)*	.044222 (.115578)	.433308 (.149574)*
YEAR	-1.062560 (.051304)*	-1.014868 (.058797)*	-.327216 (.020253)*	-.364800 (.025486)*
MISSISSIPPI-VALLEY	.171666 (1.573000)	9.571634 (1.768420)*		
SOUTHEAST	2.002043 (1.412870)	3.460663 (1.614665)		
SOUTHWEST-MOUNTAIN	-.210941 (1.326972)	-1.771281 (1.551713)		
PACIFIC	-7.206606 (1.191545)*	-8.011806 (1.355866)*		
TEAMS-CBD	4.341439 (.465389)*	8.315012 (.535374)*	1.371928 (.178445)*	3.975068 (.227118)*
TEAMS-CBD-EDGE	2.483731 (.470124)*	6.569611 (.537119)*	1.283944 (.180607)*	1.942432 (.226893)*
TEAMS-OTHER-CENTRAL-CITY	3.475913 (.318303)*	4.927645 (.362707)*	1.980020 (.129475)*	3.064189 (.162742)*
TEAMS-SUBURB	.002401 (.431908)	2.334771 (.480367)*	1.258664 (.176358)*	2.946934 (.217229)*
Constant	2083.158979	1976.119600	646.198812	706.044967
Multiple R	.86676	.87414	.83092	.84922
R Square	.75128	.76412	.69043	.72117
Adjusted R Square	.74858	.76129	.68820	.71895
Standard Error	11.43288	12.46909	4.69629	5.63573
F-ratio	278.14197	270.22311	309.17694	324.59296
Significance of F	.0000	.0000	.0000	.0000
number of cases	1118	1013	1118	1013

Standard error in parenthesis. * Means one-tailed $p < 0.01$.

Table 5–3
Two-Stage Least Squares Evaluation of Professional Team Locations and Metropolitan Share of Region Economic Activities (*Second Stage Output Reported*)

Variable and Statistic	Dependent Variable			
	TEAMS-CBD	TEAMS-CBD	TEAMS-CBD	TEAMS-CBD
MSA-SHARE-STATE-INCOME	.060172 (.006439)*			
MSA-SHARE-STATE-REC-INCOME		.044016 (.003290)*		
MSA-SHARE-REGIONAL-INCOME			.037270 (.010413)*	
MSA-SHARE-REGIONAL-REC-INCOME				.040666 (.005715)*
MSA-RATIO-PER-CAPITA-INCOME	-1.765689 (.372124)*	-2.042978 (.325248)*	.277734 (.241967)	-.165343 (.239538)
MSA-SHARE-MANUF-INCOME	-.050027 (.006609)*	-.032100 (.003588)*	-.009337 (.012248)	-.019298 (.008515)
MSA-POP-CHANGE	.010384 (.028949)	-.077166 (.027456)*	-.157283 (.019857)*	-.154814 (.020095)*
YEAR	.063731 (.008212)*	.042120 (.005289)*	.010374 (.005133)	.010928 (.004265)*
MISSISSIPPI-VALLEY	.854174 (.123884)*	.508695 (.113366)*		
SOUTHEAST	-.496646 (.116203)*	-.389106 (.106980)*		
SOUTHWEST-MOUNTAIN	-.397939 (.107067)*	-.054432 (.104458)		
PACIFIC	.148290 (.111019)	.256894 (.097580)*		
Constant	-124.753603	-81.650211	-20.426633	-21.094398
Multiple R	.49156	.57455	.35993	.42361
R Square	.24163	.33010	.12955	.17945
Adjusted R Square	.23547	.32410	.12563	.17537
Standard Error	.95641	.83930	.85145	.80384
F-ratio	39.22516	54.97084	33.09969	44.04460
Significance of F	.0000	.0000	.0000	.0000
Number of cases	1118	1013	1118	1013

Standard error in parenthesis. * Means one-tailed $p < 0.01$.

A reasonably clear pattern emerges from all equations. As a general proposition, the greatest economic benefits to the metropolitan area occur when professional sports stadia are located in the central business district. In general, the least amount of benefits accrue to those MSAs that have stadia located in the suburbs.

Share of Region Personal Income. When defining the state as the region of analysis, the greatest gains are made when sports stadia and teams playing therein are located in the CBD, followed by locations elsewhere in the central city and then by location at the CBD edge. The coefficient for suburban locations is less than one-thousandth the size of the other location-related coefficients, and insignificant in any event. When defining the region as the census region, the order of greatest benefits accruing to the MSA begin with location elsewhere in the central city followed in order by the CBD, the CBD edge, and then the suburbs.

In the analysis of MSA share of state personal income, for example, the share of the MSA's income rose on average 4.3 percent for each major league playing in the CBD, 2.5 percent for each team playing at the CBD edge, and 3.5 percent for each team playing elsewhere in the central city; there was no effect on the MSA's share of state income for major league teams playing in the suburbs. When the region is defined as the census region, an MSA's share of the census region personal income rose 8.3 percent, 6.6 percent, 4.9 percent, and 2.3 percent for each major league playing in the CBD, the CBD edge, elsewhere in the central city, and in the suburbs, respectively. General trends are evident from both analyses; central locations on the whole fare better than suburban locations.

The apparent improvement in performance of suburban location when defining the region as the census region seems incongruous with results when the region is defined as the state. Certainly by expanding the definition of "region" beyond the state, the coefficients on most location variables fall because the scale increases. (If the "region" were defined as the nation there would be no effect.) The elevated performance of the suburban location variable is explainable as a function of the level of analysis. When considering an entire census region, those MSAs taken as a whole that have professional sports attract fans from outside MSA boundaries, often across state lines (such as Kansas City attracting fans from Kansas and Iowa, and northeastern New Jersey attracting fans from New York City). Still, even with this more favorable scale of analysis, suburban locations do not influence MSA economies as much as more centralized locations.

Share of Region Recreation Personal Income. As in the analysis described above, the MSA's share of regional recreation personal income when the region is defined as the state is highest when stadia and the professional teams playing therein are located in the CBD. Location elsewhere in the central city and location at the edge of the CBD are a close second and third with suburban locations in having a negative association. An MSA's share of the state's personal income in recreation rises by 1.4 percent, 1.3 percent, 2.0 percent, and 1.3 percent for each major league team playing in the CBD, the CBD edge, elsewhere in the central city, or in the suburbs, respectively.

When the region is defined as the census region, some relationships change in very interesting but explainable ways. The greatest share of benefits accrues to MSAs when the stadia are located elsewhere in the CBD, followed distantly by locations elsewhere in the central city and the suburbs. Teams playing at the edge of CBDs had the smallest effect on recreation income. An MSA's share of the state's personal income in recreation rises by 4.0 percent, 1.9 percent, 3.1 percent, and 2.9 percent for each major league team playing in the CBD, the CBD edge, elsewhere in the central city, or in the suburbs, respectively.

One may surmise that when evaluating only recreation personal income it may not matter much where stadia are located, except that maximum benefits accrue when they are located in a CBD. This seems reasonable since (1) recreation and amusement income is usually a small share of total income in most MSAs, (2) jobs in the recreation and amusement area are the most fungible since they require few skills or literacy to perform and thus provided one has access to stadia one has the opportunity to acquire income from such service, and (3) it is the stadia themselves that generate much of the very recreation personal income reported. Thus, a stadium in the cornfields will change recreation personal income considerably over that which is observed in vacant cornfields, but a stadium located downtown does not change the CBD's total share of recreation personal income by as much.

The small effect with respect to CBD edge location is also interesting. One could suppose that if there are barriers clearly separating the edge from the CBD and even the rest of the central city, such as freeways or railroad tracks, and given that recreational income opportunities may be spread somewhat uniformly across the central city, any effect of CBD edge location on MSA recreation personal income would not be detectable through the crude measures employed in this analysis.

A Note on Other Variables. Other variables lend further insights to the analysis. The economic factor variables in all equations clearly indicate that an MSA's share of regional income will rise over time from its initial base of wealth (ratio of per capital income to region's per capital income) and manufacturing (MSA's share of region's durable goods manufacturing). This is to be expected for the simple reason that wealthier and more industrialized metropolitan areas have the resources needed to sustain growth or at least maintain relative share of regional economic activity.

The variable *YEAR* is negative and significant in all equations, indicating that in general all MSAs lost some share of regional income through the simple passage of time. This is not unexpected, because as the national population deconcentrates further those MSAs with higher shares of regional economic activity will lose some share to newly growing areas. Is this inconsistent with the economic factor variables? Not at all. Even in declining regions such as the rustbelt, MSAs with strong bases of wealth and manufacturing use their immense resources to counteract a sizeable share of potential economic leakage to other areas. Economic factors and the passage of time may have offsetting effects, but the weight of the coefficients of the economic factors indeed outweigh the time.

The regional control variables (binary or dummies) are merely controls, and so no direction of association or even expectation of significance is expected. When using the rustbelt region as the referent (with the binary or dummy variable not included in the equation), MSA share of regional income rose relative to the rustbelt in the Mississippi Valley and Southeastern regions but fell in the Southwest-Mountain and Pacific regions. This suggests that in the rustbelt, MSAs continued to hold if not expand their share of state or regional income relative to the Southwest-Mountain and Pacific regions. This is expected, since those two regions have seen considerable expansion of new development away from older MSAs into smaller and newer ones during the study period. The MSAs that dominate the Southeast continued to expand their share of state and regional income, however; this is evident with the rise of such regionally dominant MSAs as Atlanta, Charlotte, Dallas, Houston, and more recently Orlando and Tampa Bay.

Chicken-or-the-Egg Evaluation

Two-stage least squares analysis is used to test for the chicken-and-egg effect; that is, do professional sports lead to economic improvement or does economic improvement lead to professional sports. Table 5–3 shows a positive and statistically significant association between the number of teams playing in the CBD (the location that for the most part had the great influence on metropolitan economies) and the dependent variables from the first equation (Table 5–2). It would appear that it is the strength of the MSA economy either in size or in growth that attracts professional sports. This is sensible, because owners of professional sports teams are unlikely to risk millions of dollars in small markets. Since there is an interactive effect, metropolitan areas wishing to consider professional sports teams as an element of an overall economic development strategy may consider attracting teams to those areas of the MSA that generate the greatest level of interaction, which would normally be considered the CBD or other nodes of elevated activity. For brevity, only the findings from Cochrane Circuit regressions are reviewed, not the equations themselves.

Cochrane-Orcutt Evaluations

Twenty-five MSAs saw either the introduction of sports or the relocation of sports teams within them during at least four years in the study period. It is useful to summarize and interpret the meaning of the analysis for each of the MSAs here.

Atlanta. All teams played at the CBD edge, with hockey arriving in 1972 and leaving in 1981. The analysis suggests a positive association between teams playing in CBD edge facilities and the MSA's share of regional personal income.

Buffalo. The hockey team has always played downtown (so it has no "difference" effect on analysis) while the football team first played in the central city has played in a suburb since 1973. The analysis suggests that any professional team playing anywhere in the Buffalo area will have a positive effect on the MSA's share of the region's income, perhaps because within its market area there are simply so few leisure alternatives available, especially during fall and winter. Moreover, relative to other MSAs (such as Minneapolis-St.Paul), the defined MSA is much smaller in territory and several small MSAs are within easy driving distance.

Charlotte. During the study period, Charlotte received a professional basketball franchise which is located in a new stadium constructed in the central city. A positive although marginally significant statistical association[f] is seen between the MSA's share of regional personal income at the presence of a franchise playing in the central city. Charlotte's market area is widely known to include parts of other MSAs and much of the North and South Carolina hinterlands.

Cleveland. Cleveland's baseball and football teams played at the edge of the CBD during nearly the entire study period while the basketball team played in a suburb. Modest shifting of professional sports venues between the CBD, CBD edge, and a suburb indicate reasonably strong evidence that any professional team playing anywhere in the Cleveland area will have a positive effect on the MSA's share of the region's income. Like Buffalo, Cleveland's defined MSA is small and fans from several other MSAs can easily drive to and from Cleveland on game days.

Dallas. After a few years playing in the central city during the late 1960s and early 1970s, the city's notable football team plays in a suburb while its basketball and recently acquired hockey teams play at the edge of the CBD. (The baseball team essentially plays in the Fort Worth MSA, which is evaluated separately.) The analysis suggests that the teams playing at the CBD edge have no statistically significant effect on the share of the region's personal income flowing to the Dallas MSA, but relocating the football team to the suburb probably had an adverse effect since there is a statistically significant and positive income relationship for the time when it played in the central city.

Denver. Professional teams have played in Denver mostly in facilities located in the central city. Where teams have played closer in, such as the edge of the CBD, the MSA's share of the region's personal income was improved at a marginally significant level.

Detroit. During the study period, Detroit's football and basketball teams relocated to the suburbs. Statistical analysis suggests that Detroit's sports teams do not contribute significantly to the MSA's share of the region's personal income.

Hartford. During the study period, Hartford was awarded a hockey franchise, which plays in a facility in the central city. Statistical analysis suggests that Hartford's professional sports team does not contribute significantly to the MSA's share of the region's personal income. The reason may be that as the MSA's only professional sport, hockey attracts the fewest fans of the four major sports.

Indianapolis. During the study period Indianapolis gained a professional football team that plays in a facility located downtown. Its basketball team relocated from elsewhere in the central city to the CBD. Statistical analysis suggests that the MSA's share of the region's personal income is improved at a marginally significant level when teams locate in the CBD and the central city.

Los Angeles. As befitting its character, professional sports teams are sprawled throughout the Los Angeles MSA, and were divided evenly in number between the central city and suburban locations during the study period. The statistical analysis shows that where teams played in the central city, the MSA's share of the region's personal income was increased significantly.

Miami. Miami saw the introduction and relocation of its professional football teams and has recently added professional basketball and baseball teams. Statistical analysis indicates that professional sports have little influence on the share of the MSA's regional personal income. However, professional teams playing in downtown venues that were recently completed, combined with a positive albeit weakly significant association, suggests the potential for a statistically significant influence in the future.

Minneapolis. Minneapolis's professional sports teams all moved from the suburbs to the CBD during the study period. Statistical analysis suggests that Minneapolis's professional sports teams do not contribute significantly to the MSA's share of the region's personal income. Because the study area is so large, the analysis essentially internalizes the allocation of leisure resources.

New York. Two professional teams have always played in the CBD while between two and four teams have played elsewhere in the central city and another one to three teams have played in the Long Island suburbs. Because of the enormity of the New York MSA's share of regional personal income, professional sports has an inconsequential effect on the MSA's economy.

Northeastern New Jersey. One, two, three, and then four professional teams have located in northeastern New Jersey during the study period, including two football teams that play in the same stadium. The

professional facilities themselves are located in no particularly centralized place and so all are considered suburban. The teams essentially
draw from the enormity of the New York market across the Hudson River
in another MSA. A positive and statistically significant association exists
between the ratio of the Primary Metropolitan Statistical Area (PMSA)
to regional personal income, and the number of professional teams playing in suburban venues.

Anaheim-Orange County. One professional team has always
played in the Anaheim central city while first one and then two teams
played in suburban Orange County outside Anaheim. Relative to the
baseball team playing in the central city, the teams playing in suburban
Orange County appear to have no statistically significant influence on the
PMSA's share of the region's personal income.

Orlando. Orlando received its first professional team, a basketball
team, in 1989, which plays in the central city. Analysis suggests that professional sports has a positive and statistically significant influence on
the MSA's share of the region's personal income. This seems a little surprising considering the enormity of the MSA's entertainment sector.
However, the team perhaps draws more people at the margin from the
surrounding counties outside the MSA to see professional sports than
would otherwise visit amusements—and perhaps once in Orlando they
partake in those amusement opportunities.

Phoenix. Phoenix has long had a professional basketball team,
which played first in the central city and has played in the CBD since
1992. It recently acquired a football team, which plays in a suburb. Statistical analysis suggests that the MSA's share of the region's personal income is influenced positively with professional sports located in the
central city (there is too little data to confirm the effects of CBD location
on the same sport) but there is no such statistical evidence with respect to
the suburban venue.

Sacramento. Sacramento has a professional basketball team that
plays in the central city. It is notable for being considered the National
Basketball Association's most advanced stadium and one which the lu-
crative Portland basketball franchise replicated for a new stadium built
there. Oddly, the owner of the team playing in the Sacramento stadium
wants to relocate to the CBD where he may be able to sell more VIP

lounges and at higher price. As it is, there is a positive and statistically significant association between professional sports playing in the central city and the MSA's share of regional personal income.

Salt Lake City. Salt Lake City has had a professional basketball team since 1978, which initially played in a CBD venue and now plays at the edge. Statistical analysis suggests that the CBD venue was associated with the MSA receiving a lower share of regional personal income while the edge location is statistically associated, albeit marginally, with a higher share. This statistical relationship may be explained in part because the CBD location was near the tabernacle of the Church of Jesus Christ of Latter-Day Saints and also during a time in which it was more difficult to procure spirits than it is at present.

San Antonio. San Antonio has had a professional basketball team which has played there since 1972 and has always been in the CBD during the study period. Although there is not a statistically significant association between the presence of this team and the MSA's share of regional personal income, the correlation is positive nonetheless.

Seattle. Seattle has steadily added professional sports teams since the late 1960s but they are all located in the CBD (albeit some distance from commonly accepted city centers but nonetheless within easy walking distance without barriers from many pre- and postgame CBD destinations). The association between the MSA's share of regional personal income and the number of sports teams playing in the CBD is positive and significant.

Springfield. Springfield saw only five years of professional sports, all of which were played in the central city. Despite just a few years of professional sports-playing in Springfield, there is a positive and statistically significant association between those sports and the MSA's share of regional personal income.

St. Louis. St. Louis's professional sports teams have always played in the CBD but their number has varied with the most recent movement of the city's football team to Phoenix. There is a reasonable albeit marginal statistically significant association between the number of professional sports teams playing in the CBD and the MSA's share of regional income.

Tampa Bay. Tampa Bay had a football team for most of the study period and it recently added a baseball team. Both play in central city locations. However, statistical analysis indicates no significant association between professional teams playing in those venues and the MSA's share of regional personal income.

Washington, D.C. Through the study period, Washington, D.C. has had one professional team playing in the central city, but all other teams play in the suburbs. Professional teams playing in suburban venues do not contribute in a statistically significant way with the MSA's share of regional income.

These analyses of individual MSAs suggest that effects of professional sports, in general, and the location of their venues in particular depend on the size of the MSA's economy and its territorial reach. Thus, professional sports in New York has an inconsequential effect on that MSA's economy because of the sheer size of its economy, and is also an inconsequential effect on the Minneapolis-St. Paul economy because its MSA boundaries absorb nearly the entire market area of professional teams playing there.

On the other hand, when looking at MSAs with territory that is not large, such as Indianapolis (3,000+ square miles), Seattle (less than 2,000 square miles after adjusting for federally owned land), and Denver (less than 3,000 square miles after adjusting for federally owned land), a general pattern emerges: The closer professional teams play to the center of the city the greater the apparent economic effect. Thus when professional sports are played in the city of Los Angeles proper, Orlando, Seattle, and other cities with small MSA boundaries relative to their markets, such teams will have a positive effect on the MSA's economy. With some exceptions, such as Buffalo, this effect tends to diminish as sports venues are located farther away.

CONCLUSIONS AND POLICY IMPLICATIONS

The analysis contributes to the debate on professional sports stadia investment. It is suggested that if the decision has been made to construct a professional sports stadium to keep or lure a professional sports team, locating such a facility in the CBD, at the edge of the CBD, or elsewhere in the central city will probably generate greater economic benefits than locating it in suburbs. The research reported here suggests that the largest share of benefits should accrue to MSAs when such facilities are located in or close to the CBD.

This is not to say that public investments in such facilities are prudent, considering their opportunity costs. The region may be worse off if hundreds of millions of dollars in scarce public resources are siphoned away from more productive investments or even tax cuts.

A word is needed about the potentially contradictory results presented by the analysis of recreation personal income. The analysis should not be seen as suggesting that benefits are greatest when locating sports stadia elsewhere in the central city or in a suburb—which in either case implies a non-central location. That such location options may generate greater increases in recreation personal income than alternative locations is reasonable, but an economic development strategy that focuses solely on this relationship will miss the interactive effect stadia may have on other economic sectors. For example, a stockholder in the Cincinnati Reds baseball franchise informed this writer that the city has decided to build two new stadia to replace Riverfront Stadium but that all new stadia would be located either in the CBD or its edge. He indicated that the city has learned that Riverfront Stadium events attract several thousand people from out of town. Many of them not only watch a game, but they stay in downtown hotels (Standard Industrial Classification [SIC] 70), shop at local stores (SIC 56, 57, 59), eat and drink at local restaurants (SIC 58), go to beauty salons (SIC 72), and visit other local attractions such as museums and art galleries (SIC 84).

Implications for Federal Policy

It is difficult to get a clear picture of how federal policy influences major league sports stadia construction or how it can influence those decisions during a time of federal retrenchment from involvement in local affairs. Subsidies for sports stadia construction and operation tend to be a strictly local affair. Gone are the federal programs that facilitated stadium construction efforts, including use of federal urban renewal funds to acquire and redevelop land, federal exemption of taxes due on income from industrial development revenue bonds, and federal low-interest loans or grants for upgrading infrastructure. There are nonetheless several important federal policy levers. Should Congress decide that as a matter of national interest the revitalization of central cities through the construction of major league sports stadia is expedient (and perhaps all other related public-gathering venues such as convention centers and exhibition halls), it may consider a number of adjustments to current federal policies.

Since 1986, earnings from the "private" use of industrial development revenue bonds has not enjoyed exemption from federal (and often state) income taxation. However, where general obligation, revenue bonds, or tax increment bonds are issued by states and authorized local governments for public purposes, which may include publicly financed stadia if they remain publicly owned, earnings may be exempt. For example, the Georgia Dome in Atlanta was financed by state-issued revenue bonds, Camden Yard in Baltimore was financed through state-issued general obligation bonds, and Salt Lake City's Delta Center was financed from city-issued tax increment financing bonds. In all cases, owners of bonds are exempt from paying federal taxes on interest earned from bond yields (as well as state taxes if they live in those respective states). In all cases, the stadia were built in centralized locations. There is nothing to prevent states and local governments from using federal tax exemption to locate new stadia in suburban areas, however. In an effort to stimulate economic development of central cities, for example, Congress may consider limiting the use of federally tax exempt bond issues for stadia and related facilities to central cities.

The role of transportation investments cannot be ignored. Many suburban sports stadia are made possible through the construction of new roads, widening of existing roads, and installation of interchanges or intersections—often using federal funds in whole or in part. Congress may consider limiting the use of federal highway funds for these purposes if indeed it decides—as evidence suggests—that construction of centrally located sports stadia does more to advance regional economic activity than the construction of such facilities elsewhere.

Related to transportation issues, the federal Transportation Efficiency Act for the 21st Century (ISTEA), which is up for renewal by Congress, may be used to improve access to centrally located stadia and to improve the pedestrian connections between those stadia and nearby activity centers such as downtowns.

The federal government, chiefly through the U.S. Department of Housing and Urban Development (HUD), has a number of programs aimed at improving blighted or deteriorating central city areas. Some of these programs are competitive in nature, such as the recently implemented empowerment zone programs. One criterion that may be considered in competition for access to such federal funds may be the proximity or accessibility of stadia to those areas.

Finally, the power of persuasion cannot be understated. Through support of research, workshops, demonstrations, and a variety of educational initiatives the federal government, again perhaps chiefly through HUD, may influence local decision-making in choosing where to make the next round of sports stadia investments. It is perhaps this latter effort that may prove to be more effective since the other efforts require significant and potentially controversial changes to existing federal policies. It is also perhaps the least intrusive into local decision-making processes.

Parting Comment

The bottom line reached through analysis is that where total economic benefits are the criterion for making large public investments and where a decision has been made to facilitate construction of a professional sports stadium, the best place in which to locate that facility is in the central business district, with a close second being the edge of the CBD.

REFERENCES

Abbott, C. 1993. Five downtown strategies: policy discourse and downtown planning since 1945. *Journal of Policy History*, 5, 1: 5–27.

Baade, R. A. 1994. Stadiums, professional sports, and economic development: Assessing the reality. *Heartland Policy Study*, 62, March 28.

Baade, R. A. 1996. Professional sports as catalysts for metropolitan economic development. *Journal of Urban Affairs* 18, 1: 1–17.

Baade, R. A. 1997. Stadiums, professional sports, and city economics: An analysis of the United States experience. In *The stadium and the city,* J. Bale and O. Moen, (eds.). Keele, England: Keele University Press.

Baade, R. A. and R. F. Dye. 1988. Sports stadiums and area development: A critical review. *Economic Development Quarterly*, 2: 265–275.

Baade, R. A. and R. F. Dye. 1990. The impact of stadiums and professional sports on metropolitan area development. *Growth and Change*, 21: 1–14.

Baim, D. 1990. Sports stadiums as wise investments: An evaluation. Detroit: Heartland Institute Policy Study, No. 32, November.

Baim, D. 1992. *The sports stadium as a municipal investment*. Westport, CT: Greenwood Press.

Beauregard, R. A. 1986. Urban form and the redevelopment of central business districts. *Journal of Architectural and Planning Research*, 3, 2: 183–198.

Brooks, J. S. and A. H. Young. 1993. Revitalizing the central business district in the face of decline: The case of New Orleans, 1973–1993. *Town Planning Review 64,* 3:251–271.

Bureau of Economic Analysis. 1977. *BEA Economic Areas*. Washington, DC: U.S. Department of Commerce.

Deloitte and Touche. 1993. *Economic impact study of a major league baseball stadium and franchise*, December. Phoenix: Deloitte and Touche.

Euchner, C. C. 1993. *Playing the field: Why sports teams move and cities fight to keep them.* Baltimore: Johns Hopkins University Press.

Frieden, B. J. and L. B. Sagalyn. 1989. *Downtown, Inc.* Cambridge: The MIT Press.

Greco, A. L. 1994. Sports value more myth than reality. *Standard and Poor's Creditweek*, July 26.

Jacobs, J. 1961. *The Death and Life of Great American Cities.* New York: Vintage Books.

McBee, S. 1992. *Downtown Development Handbook*, second edition. Washington, DC: Urban Land Institute.

Mills, E. S. 1993. The misuse of regional economic models. *Cato Journal*, 13.

Nebel, E. C. III et al. 1986. *The economic impact of the Louisiana superdome (1975–1985).* New Orleans: University of New Orleans, College of Business.

Noll, R. G. 1974. Attendance and price setting. In *Government and the sports business*, R.G. Noll (ed.). Washington, D.C.: Brookings Institute, pp. 115–157.

Northeastern Illinois Planning Commission. 1986. *A Comparative Guide to Northeastern Illinois and 25 Other Metropolitan Areas.* DeKalb, IL: Northern Illinois University, Center for Government Studies, June.

Norton, E. 1993. Football at any cost: one city's mad chase for an NFL franchise. *Wall Street Journal*, October 13.

Okner, B. A. 1974. Subsidies of stadiums and arenas. In *Government and the sports business*, R.G. Noll, (ed.). Washington, DC: Brookings Institute, pp. 325–347.

Peterson, David C. 1996. *Sports, Convention, and Entertainment Facilities.* Washington, DC: Urban Land Institute.

Quirk, J. P. 1987. The quirk study: A close look at the two proposals. *St. Louis Post Dispatch*, January 18, pp. 5i, 8i.

Quirk, J. P. and R. D. Fort. 1992. *Pay dirt: the business of professional team sports.* Princeton: Princeton University Press.

Rosentraub, M. S. and S. Nunn. 1978. Suburban city investment in professional sports. *American Behavioral Scientist* 21:393–414.

Rosentraub, M. S., D. Swindell, M. Przybylski, and D. R. Mullins. 1994. Sport and downtown development strategy: if you build it, will jobs come? *Journal of Urban Affairs* 16: 221–239.

NOTES

[a]Provided significance is established at the 0.10 level of the one-tailed t-test or the 0.20 level of the two-tailed t-test, either of which may be appropriate levels considering the small sample size.

[b]Baade's work does not include Denver's Coors Field, a recently constructed stadium at the edge of the CBD.

[c]This excludes Omaha, Nebraska, which shared home basketball games with Kansas City during one year but includes Springfield, Massachusetts, which hosted the Hartford Whaler hockey team during the two years in which the Hartford Civic Center Coliseum was rebuilt after its roof collapsed.

[d]The Bureau of Economic Analysis suppresses reporting of SIC 79 data for seven MSAs for multiple years (Cincinnati, Cleveland, Kansas City, Minneapolis-St. Paul, New Haven, Orlando, and Springfield).

[e]There was a moderately high correlation between state or regional personal income or recreation income and the ratio of MSA per capita income to the state or region per capita income. This is not unexpected and does not change the outcome when removed from the equation.

[f]I use the term "marginally significant" to convey that the statistical association falls outside the customary maximum of $p < 0.10$ level of the one-tailed t-test (if direction is predicted) but within about $p < 0.25$.

CHAPTER 6

Conclusion:
Summary and Future Research

FRITZ W. WAGNER, TIMOTHY E. JODER,
AND ANTHONY J. MUMPHREY JR.

Becker and Collins, in Chapter 1, put forward the concept of privatism to characterize urban development policy. Privatism has generally been defined as the set of place-based strategies provided by government (federal, state, and local) to increase the exchange value of the central city for the benefit of the business elite. However, policies that promote the private city, emphasizing growth over equity, could negatively affect some socioeconomic groups more than others (Wong 1990; Young, Whelan, and Lauria 1995).

Of course, who or what is affected depends upon the specific issue and the local government's policy decision. For example, in Rockford, Illinois, the political leadership initially favored lowering taxes to lure industry but found that funding for schools declined as a consequence (Logan and Molotch 1987:16). Municipalities whose economic development policies focus on growth for the sake of growth encounter many problems, among them urban sprawl and unfocused investment. Is the promise of positive impacts from a development project real, or mere hyperbole? Given reduced state funding and the federal government's virtual abandonment of central cities, decision makers need to manage the central city's capital resources more effectively and efficiently.

One recent growth strategy for revitalizing downtown and the central city, following the principle of the more investments made the better, has been to attract and invest in gambling casinos (Hernon 1994; Rich 1990). While casinos may be part of a general growth strategy, they should not be the centerpieces of a development strategy. In other words, communities should not attract or invest in "glitter" and "dazzle" with the expectation of economic revitalization (Rubenstein 1984; Gross 1998). Despite all the talk about how much revenue a growth industry could generate, local governments need to consider the impacts on the community and how "real" those impacts are. Monti and Goodman, in Chapter 2, found that large multiuse stadium complexes, based on the experiences of Atlanta and New Orleans, contributed little to the social vitality of the neighborhoods in which those complexes were located. Thus, while economic growth is essential for the basic survival of communities, community leaders should emphasize development. In this book we focused on some successful development strategies.

SUMMARY

The authors in this collection reviewed three strategies for managing the central city's capital resources in light of reduced federal and state spending. These strategies involved (1) reusing temporarily obsolete abandoned and derelict structures, (2) establishing business improvement districts, and (3) siting sports stadia. Each strategy required cooperation among municipalities, businesses, nonprofit organizations, and community residents. Moreover, each strategy enhanced use values as well as increased exchange values. Based on the case study research presented here, we conclude that in a postfederal environment, five factors are advisable for successful central city revitalization:

1. Develop public–private partnerships.
2. Commit to physical revitalization to improve quality of life among central city residents.
3. Take a holistic view and focus on benefits to the entire region rather than on a single area.
4. Involve all actors—public, private, and community residents— in the planning process.
5. Craft strategies that take advantage of the unique strengths of each central city.

Develop Public–Private Partnerships.

Elise Bright, in Chapter 3, demonstrated the need to work with government agencies in order to accomplish revitalization goals. Most temporarily obsolete abandoned derelict structures (TOADS) become potential tools for urban revitalization as a result of government action.

These actions include: delinquent tax seizures, abandoned urban renewal efforts, HUD foreclosures, Resolution Trust Corporation reversions, military base closings, school closings, abandoned rights of way, and various other forms of public condemnation. Once the structures become government property, they tend to languish and serve no useful purpose. However, once private actors such as developers, lenders, and community development corporations become involved, they are able to form partnerships with the public agencies in order to put TOADS to productive use. Edward Rogowsky and Jill Gross (Chapter 4) point out that business improvement districts (BIDs) represent a particular form of partnership between city government and local property owners. While the need for a business improvement district may come from private, public, or nonprofit actors, day-to-day decision-making is dominated by private property owners who finance the partnership through a mutually agreed upon supplementary property tax assessment.

Commit to Physical Revitalization for Improving the Quality of Life among Central City Residents

All four studies in this volume emphasize this lesson. Monti and Goodman (Chapter 2), in particular, showed that it is not enough simply to offer social programs in an attempt to raise the standard of living in a community. Long-lasting effects will only come about if the physical environment of the residents is improved along with the cultural and social environment. In her analysis of TOADS in Seattle, Bright found that surplus land near I–90 was successfully developed with single and duplex housing for low- and moderate-income first-time home buyers. Rogowsky and Gross (Chapter 4) discovered that business improvement districts appear to create safer environments and also seem to increase shopping activity. Nelson (Chapter 5) measured the effects that physical development can have on a community. His analysis found that the effect of sports stadia development on the central city varies from city to city.

Take a Holistic View toward Urban Revitalization

In order for revitalization projects to be successful, it is necessary that they benefit the entire region, not just a single neighborhood. If the project benefits the region, then regional actors from all sectors of the community will be more inclined to get involved and support the project. In the case of TOADS, Bright points out that regional cooperation was often present and took many forms, including cooperative TOADS reuse programs, tax base sharing, cooperation among boroughs, growth management, and regional provision of infrastructure and transit. Rogowsky and Gross argue that the broad holistic view is both beneficial and necessary in order for business improvement districts to succeed. Corporate and main street business improvement districts, for example, could attract new businesses to the central city and prevent existing businesses from leaving the central city. Furthermore, the success of a business improvement district could spur redevelopment in adjacent areas. In addition to policy considerations, there are also political realities. One such reality is gaining support from the mayor, city council, and other political leaders. If a development project does not benefit the entire central city or region, it is unlikely to get the support of political actors from outside the development area. This lack of support will likely doom the project. Nelson points out that the positive effect of strong political support is especially evident when dealing with large multiuse structures.

Involve All Actors in the Planning Process

Monti and Goodman characterized development strategies as either active or supportive. When public agencies take the initiative in a development project, then that strategy is "active"; when the private sector or nonprofit sector takes the initiative, then that strategy is "supportive." Whether active or supportive, these strategies bring all members of the community into the planning process. For example, it is essential to plan for the reuse of TOADS by involving the residents of the neighborhoods in which these properties are located. Where this has occurred projects have been successful, particularly in Boston and Cleveland. Residents provide continuity; they have a vested interest in seeing the project completed. Their role is particularly important when projects take longer than expected. A development project that spans several years encounters frequent changes in the political administration and thus a loss of institutional memory. Bright also shows that redeveloping abandoned property requires local government to relax some regulations and also to offer incentives to the private sector.

While the success of redeveloping TOADS rests on the interaction among government, residents, and the private and not-for-profit sectors, a successful business improvement district results from the interaction between the business community and the government. Business improvement districts are usually requested by local merchants who seek better services than those provided by the city. These merchants also anticipate increased sales from establishing such a district. City governments find that BIDs reduce maintenance and capital improvement costs. Thus, a local government's responsibilities are to approve BID boundaries, approve the funding strategy, and adopt the proposed budget.

Take Advantage of the Central City's Unique Strengths

Nelson (Chapter 5) demonstrated that some cities are better situated to take advantage of sports stadia than others. Much depends on the cultural and hospitality enterprises that already exist in the central city before the stadium is built. Simply building a stadium in an economically depressed area is unlikely to have much of a positive effect since sports fans will attend the sporting event and then depart from the area without spending any more money. However, if the stadium is constructed in an area where there are other economic venues such as hotels, restaurants, and nightclubs, sports fans are more likely to spend more money in the area.

Bright (Chapter 3) discovered that the successful reuse of TOADS is dependent upon that property's proximity to other successful—usually commercial—development projects. Rogowsky and Gross (Chapter 4) show that one reason for the success of corporate and main street BIDs in New York City was the unique financial opportunities available in that city. While BIDs are one economic development strategy for managing the central city's capital resources, they may not prove successful in every central city. Cities need access to similar types of financial assistance. New York City has thirty-nine BIDs, whereas New Orleans has only one, which is a corporate-type BID. Monti and Goodman (Chapter 2) show it is necessary to match the specific development strategy with the specific type of neighborhood. That is to say, the socioeconomic characteristics of the neighborhood dictate whether active strategies involving public agencies prove successful or whether supportive strategies involving the private sector prove more successful. There is no simple formula—these decisions must be made on a case by case basis.

All five lessons presented above contribute to successful revitalization efforts. However, these lessons should not be generalized to all cities and all circumstances. This set of case studies and the lessons learned from them builds on previous research. Contemporary urban problems can only be solved by applying research to specific conditions and learning what works and what does not on a case by case basis. An incremental building process allows us to formulate specific hypotheses and test them empirically. It is from these empirically tested hypotheses that generalized solutions to urban decay can be formulated and transformed into practical policy recommendations.

COMMENT ON URBAN POLICY

The riots in South-Central Los Angeles in the spring of 1992 led many political leaders and urbanists to assert that the number of urban programs and the amount of public dollars invested in our nation's central cities would parallel the commitment of the 1960s. However, that hope—that we as a nation would do something to revitalize the central city and uplift our poorest citizens—dissipated. The need for federal action was replaced by the performance of a robust national economy, and expectations of a general improvement.

Strategies to revitalize the central city exist, but they are not necessarily national or even statewide in scope. As our colleagues have reported, strategies are locally based and designed by municipalities in collaboration with the business community, nonprofit organizations, and community residents. The goal of most of these revitalization strategies is to manage the central city's capital resources effectively. In this book, three specific examples were considered: reusing temporarily obsolete derelict structures, establishing business improvement districts, and siting sports stadia. We contend that future urban revitalization policies and programs will come from local experiments. Thus, seeking out such experiments, analyzing them, and reporting on them to the public is a must. However, in the past, these efforts have been largely uncoordinated.

The National Center for the Revitalization of Central Cities is one of the few university-based urban research consortiums in the country that is sponsored by the U.S. Congress and dedicated to central city revitalization. This consortium of academic institutions analyzes critical problems affecting America's central cities, evaluates redevelopment strategies to address those problems, and prescribes policy alternatives. To achieve its goals, the National Center has spent the past several years developing a solid base of research.

Between 1992 and 1994, National Center research teams examined the successes and failures of well-established federal and state economic development grant programs and policies. Between 1995 and 1998, National Center researchers analyzed examples of human capital investment for revitalizing central cities and examples of managing capital resources. With refunding from Congress and support from the U.S. Department of Housing and Urban Development, the National Center continues to build on its accomplishments. And as this decade ends and a new century begins, we will be on the threshold of making policy recommendations and proposing national urban redevelopment strategies.

FUTURE RESEARCH ENDEAVORS

The National Center pursues research projects in five general areas of study: economic development, housing/community development, environmental management, public finance, and information technology. Specific research projects under review include the following:

1. Measuring the feasiblility and benefits of mixed-income housing.
2. Analyzing the effects of change in neighborhood retail and service establishments on the central city.
3. Analyzing the role of housing foreclosures in shaping the urban landscape.
4. Measuring change in residential investment patterns.
5. Measuring the effects of building code enforcement on central city revitalization.
6. Evaluating the effects of empowerment zones on economic opportunity.
7. Managing brownfields as community assets.
8. Evaluating payments-in-lieu-of-taxes as a revenue-generating strategy.
9. Analyzing the monetary and nonmonetary consequences of urban sprawl and evaluating strategies for containment, including smart growth initiatives.
10. Assessing the economic benefits of historic preservation and cultural tourism for inner-city neighborhood revitalization.
11. Developing a brownfields data inventory, monitoring, and mapping system.
12. Designing microenterprise program.

REFERENCES

Gross, M. 1998. Legal gambling as a strategy for economic development. *Economic Development Quarterly*. 12(3): 203–213.

Hernon, J. 1994. Riverboat gaming bonanza. *Real Estate Review*, 24(2):40–44.

Logan, J. and H. Molotch. 1987. *Urban Fortunes: The Political Economy of Place*. Los Angeles: University of California Press.

Rich, W. 1990. Politics of casino gambling: Detroit style. *Urban Affairs Quarterly*. 26(2): 274–298.

Rubenstein, A. 1984. Casino gambling in Atlantic City: issues of development and redevelopment. *Annals of the American Political and Social Sciences*. 474: 45–59.

Wong, K. 1990. *City Choices: Education and Housing*. Albany: State University of New York Press.

Young, A., R. Whelan, and M. Lauria. 1995. The revitalization of New Orleans. In *Urban Revitalization: Policies and Programs*. Wagner, F., T. Joder, and A. Mumphrey (eds). Thousand Oaks, CA: Sage Publications.

About the Editors

Fritz W. Wagner is professor of urban and regional planning and dean of the College of Urban and Public Affairs at the University of New Orleans. B.S., Michigan State University; M.S., Ph.D. (planning), University of Washington. Wagner also serves as director of the National Center for the Revitalization of Central Cities, and the World Health Organization Collaborating Center for Health Aspects of Urban Development. His areas of interest include small-town and neighborhood planning, environmental planning, land use and zoning, policy evaluation, and planning issues in developing countries. His recent publications include "Protecting Tourists from Death and Injury in Hurricanes and Other Natural Disasters" (with R. Burby), *Disasters* (1996); *Urban Revitalization: Policies and Programs* (with T. Joder and A. Mumphrey) Sage Publications, 1995. Dr. Wagner is currently on a six-month Fulbright in Alexandria, Egypt.

Timothy E. Joder is director of sponsored research and business affairs for the College of Urban and Public Affairs at the University of New Orleans. Concurrently, he serves as deputy director of the National Center for the Revitalization of Central Cities. Prior to joining the University of New Orleans in 1981, he served as chief planner, State Planning Office, Office of the Governor of Louisiana; as a community development planner with the city of Baton Rouge and East Baton Rouge Parish; and as a coordinator of the Boca Raton, Florida, Community Development Block Grant program. He holds a bachelor of arts degree in urban affairs/geography from the University of Pittsburgh and a master's degree in public administration from the University of New Orleans. He is coeditor with Fritz Wagner of *Urban Revitalization: Programs and Policies* (1995).

Anthony J. Mumphrey Jr. is professor of urban and regional planning and research director of the National Center for the Revitalization of Central Cities at the University of New Orleans. B.S., M.S. (civil engineering), Tulane University; M.A., Ph.D. (regional science), University of Pennsylvania. Mumphrey served as executive assistant for planning and development to the mayor of New Orleans (1978 to 1984); he subsequently started a professional consulting firm that specializes in urban and regional planning, airport planning, and municipal finance. Dr. Mumphrey's research interests include creative public finance techniques, solid waste management, the impacts of annexation and defensive incorporation, city-suburban development relationships, and the decision-making process in the public sector. He recently coauthored "The Suburban Dependency Hypothesis, Reconsidered" (Journal of Planning Literature 1998, vol. 13, no. 2: 147–157). He is also coeditor of *Urban Revitalization: Policies and Programs* (with F. Wagner and T. Joder), Sage Publications, 1995.

About the Contributors

Robert Becker is the vice president of planning and operations for the Audubon Institute in New Orleans. He is also an adjunct professor at the College of Urban and Public Affairs, University of New Orleans, where he has taught since 1981. He served as executive director of the New Orleans City Planning Commission from 1982 to 1988. Since 1971, he has been associated with planning and development activities in the city of New Orleans. Mr. Becker received his bachelors degree from the State University of New York at Buffalo and his master's degree from the University of Iowa. He is a member of the American Institute of Certified Planners and the American Planning Association.

Elise Bright is an associate professor at the School of Urban and Public Affairs at the University of Texas, Arlington. She completed her undergraduate work at the University of Arizona, earned her master's degree in city planning from Harvard University in 1975 and her doctorate from Texas A&M University in 1980. She has worked in city and regional planning positions throughout the United States and has also conducted research in Europe. She joined the University of Texas, Arlington faculty in 1988, where she specializes in economic development, zoning, and environmental planning. Her current research focuses on the effects of property assessment and tax collection methods on ownership in low-income neighborhoods and the unmet housing needs of nonnuclear families.

Robert A. Collins is a doctoral student in the urban studies program at the College of Urban and Public Affairs at the University of New Orleans.

He is also a research assistant with the National Center for the Revitalization of Central Cities. Robert Collins has previously served as field assistant to former U.S. Senator J. Bennett Johnston. He has also worked on the staffs of several elected and appointed public officials including the Louisiana secretary of commerce, the Louisiana secretary of transportation and development, and U.S. Senator John Breaux. His current research interests include urban politics, cultural preservation, and ethnographic field methodology.

Michael Goodman is a research associate with the Worcester Muncipal Research Bureau in Worcester, Massachusettes. Dr. Goodman received his Ph.D. in sociology from Boston University. His research interests focus on formal and complex organizations, urban education, community development, and sociological theory.

Jill Simone Gross is an assistant professor at Hunter College in the urban planning department. She received her Ph.D. in political science from the City University of New York graduate school. She received her master's degree in 1991 from the London School of Economics and Political Science in London, England. She received her undergraduate degree from the State University of New York at Cortland in 1984. Her research interests focus on urban politics, urban political participation, and metropolitan governance structures.

Daniel Monti is associate professor of sociology at Boston University. His research interests focus on urban sociology and race and ethnic relations. He has authored or coauthored several papers and articles, and has prepared technical reports for the Urban Institute. His most recent book is *Race Redevelopment and the New Company Town* (1990).

Arthur C. Nelson is professor of city planning, public policy, and international affairs at the Georgia Institute of Technology, and currently serves as senior research fellow to the National Center for the Revitalization of Central Cities. He is widely published in the areas of regional development planning, urban form, resource land preservation, infrastructure planning and finance, growth management, and urban revitalization. He serves as an editor of the *Journal of the American Planning Association* and as associate editor of the *Journal of Urban Affairs*. He has consulted for numerous government agencies, corporations, development industry associations, and public policy associations. He earned his Ph.D. from Portland State University in regional science and regional planning. Prior to his appointment at Georgia Tech, he served on the faculties of Kansas State University and the University of New Orleans.

Edward T. Rogowsky is professor emeritus of political science at Brooklyn College, City University of New York. He directs the college's off-campus graduate center worker education program and undergraduate internship programs. He has written several books and numerous articles on urban affairs. He has served on the New York City Planning Commission. Dr. Rogowsky also hosts a weekly urban affairs program, MetroView, broadcast on CUNY-TV.

Index

Abandonment, tax delinquency
and house, 46
Age composition, redevelopment
and, 23–24
Aid to Families with Dependent
Children (AFDC), 9
American Institute of Archi-
tects, 8
Anaheim-Orange County, 138
Atlanta, Georgia
sports in, 135
Underground Atlanta project,
26–28
World Congress Center project,
28–29
Atlanta Braves Baseball Club, 117

Baade, R.A., 119–120, 121, 123,
125
Barkan, Janet, 105
Beam, John, 85, 86
Beauregard, R., 3, 4
Bingham, R., 11
Boston's Dudley Street Neighbor-
hood Initiative (DSNI) project,
52–54

Bowman, A., 2
Brooklyn
Fulton Mall, 94, 95–96
Metrotech, 96–97
Buffalo, 135
*Business Elites and Urban
Development* (Cummings), 7
Business Improvement Districts
(BIDs), 149
See also New York City,
business improvement
districts (BIDs) in
background, 82–83
common elements of, 84
community, 87
corporate, 85–86
main street, 86–87
national perspective, 83–84
typology of, 85–87

Capital, defined, 3
Central city, defined, 4
Central city revitalization,
defined, 4
Charlotte, 135–136
Chudacoff, H., 8

Cisneros, H., 5
City and Regime (Elkin), 7
*City Politics: Private Power and
    Public Policy* (Judd and
    Swanstrom), 7
Clearance projects, 8
Cleveland
    Land Reutilization Authority
        (LRA) and Cleveland Land
        Bank project, 54–57
    sports in, 136
Community-based organizations
    (CBOs), 62
Community business improvement
    districts, 87
Community Development Block
    Grants (CDBGs) (1974),
    9–10, 55, 81
Community Development
    Corporations (CDCs), 54,
    55, 57
Community Reinvestment Act
    (CRA) (1977), 56, 64
    Pittsburgh and the, 58
Comprehensive Employment and
    Training Act (CETA) (1973),
    9–10
Corporate business improvement
    districts, 85–86
Coward, Joyce, 106
Cummings, Scott, 7

Dallas, 136
Deller, Thomas, 60
Deloitte and Touche, 119
Demonstration Cities and Metro-
    politan Development Act
    (1966), 9
Denver, 136
Detroit, 136
District Management Association
    (DMA), 89

Downtown Development
    District (DDD) project,
    35–37, 85
Dudley Street Neighborhood Initia-
    tive (DSNI) project, 52–54
Dye, R.F., 121

Economic development, defined, 3
Educational levels, redevelopment
    and, 25
Elkin, Stephen, 7
Empowerment zones, 11
    basic components of, 11
Enterprise zones, 11
Exchange value, defined, 3

Federal Housing Act (1949), 8
Financing Economic Development
    (Bingham), 11
Food Stamps, 9
Ford Foundation, 53
Fulton Mall, 94, 95–96

Gambling casinos, 147–148
Gertz, Jerry, 98
Grand Central Partnership, 85
Greenberg, Michael R., 45, 46, 47,
    51

Hartford, 136
Head Start, 9
Hennepin County Government
    Center project, 30–32
Hill, E., 11
Holcomb, B., 4
Homesight, 61
Hoosier Dome, 119, 121
Hopper, Leonard, 57–58
Housing units, redevelopment
    and occupied versus vacant,
    26
Houstoun, Lawrence, Jr., 84

Imbroscio, D., 12
Income levels, redevelopment and, 25–26
Indianapolis, 137
Integration, use of term, 22–23
Intermodal Surface Transporta
tion Efficiency Act (ISTEA), 142

Jamaica Center and 165th Street Mall, 94–95, 97–99
Joder, T., 11
Johnson, Lyndon, 9
Judd, D., 7, 10, 11
Judkins-Rejected area, 60–61

Kleinberg, B., 8

Lemann, N., 9
Loring Park Development District, 30
Los Angeles, 137
Louisiana Superdome project, 37–39

MacDonald, Heather, 85
Main street business improvement districts, 86–87
Managing capital resources, de-fined, 2–3
Marino, Dennis R., 46, 61–62
Market Square Arena, 119, 121
McGuigan, Patrick, 58
McNamara, Nora, 55, 56
Medicaid, 9
Medoff, Peter, 52
Metrotech, 96–97
Miami, 137
Millard, Charles, 101
Minneapolis
  Hennepin County Government Center project, 30–32

Loring Park Development District, 30
  sports in, 137
Model Cities project, 9
Mumphrey, A., 11

National Center for the Revitaliza-tion of Central Cities (NCRCC), 20–21, 152, 153
National League of Cities, 7
New Jersey, 137–138
New Orleans
  Downtown Development District (DDD) project, 35–37, 85
  Louisiana Superdome project, 37–39
  Superdome, 119
New Urban Reality, The (Peter-son), 5
New York City, business improve-ment districts (BIDs) in, 81
  background, 82–83
  Brooklyn's Fulton Mall, 94, 95–96
  Brooklyn's Metrotech, 96–97
  conclusions and recommenda-tions, 107–110
  description of, 87–93
  effectiveness of, 99–107
  list of interviewees, 114–115
  national perspective, 83–84
  Queens' Jamaica Center and 165th Street Mall, 94–95, 97–99
  sports in, 137
  typology of, 85–87
New York City, revitalization in, 57–58

Occupational composition, rede-velopment and, 24–25

Oregon Convention Center project,
    32–34
Orlando, 138

Papano, M., 2
People-based strategies, 5, 6–7
Peterson, P., 5, 6
Philadelphia Center District BID,
    85
Phoenix, 138
Pike Place Market, 60
Pittsburgh and the CRA, 58
Place-based strategies, 5, 7
Popper, Frank J., 45, 46, 47, 51
Portland, Oregon
    Oregon Convention Center
        project, 32–34
    Portland Transit Mall and MAX
        project, 34–35
Powell, Matthew, 58, 59–60
Private City, The (Warner), 3
Privatism
    defined, 3–4, 147
    literature on, 7
Providence, revitalization in,
    58–60
Public capital, defined, 2

Quality of life, defined, 47, 49,
    149
Queens' Jamaica Center and 165th
    Street Mall, 94–95, 97–99

Racial categories, used in redevel-
    opment study, 23
*Reconstructing City Politics:
    Alternative Economic Devel-
    opment and Urban Regimes*
    (Imbroscio), 12
*Regime Politics: Governing At-
    lanta* (Stone), 7
Resolution Trust Corp., (RTC), 46,
    149

Revitalization, defined, 47
Riley Foundation, 53–54
Riots, 152
Rockford, Illinois, 147
Rosentraub, M.S., 119, 121
Rosser, Lawrence B., 46, 61–62
Rozran, Andrea R., 46, 61–62

Sacramento, 138–139
St. Louis, 139
Salt Lake City, 139
San Antonio, 139
San Diego's Jack Murphy Sta-
    dium, 120
Schwartz, Alex, 57
Seattle
    revitalization in, 60–61
    sports in, 139
Sekera, J., 10
Sklar, Holly, 52
Smith, J., 8
Special Assessment District
    (SADs), 82, 87–88
Sports stadia, role of
    Cochrane-Orcutt evaluation,
        135–140
    conclusions, 140–143
    cross-section evaluation,
        129–130, 132
    debate on the efficacy of,
        117–118
    economic factors, 122
    evaluation, 127–129, 134–140
    literature review, 118–121
    location of, importance of,
        120–127
    metropolitan areas with profes-
        sional sports franchises,
        126–127
    results and interpretations,
        129–134
    share of region personal income,
        132

share of region recreation personal income, 133
two-stage least squares evaluation, 131, 134–135
Springfield, 139
Squires, G., 3–4
Stone, Clarence, 7
Success, defined, 47–48
Swanstrom, T., 7, 10, 11
Sweeney, Michael, 56–57

Tampa Bay, 140
Tax delinquency, house abandonment and, 46
Teaford, J., 5
TOADS (temporarily, obsolete, abandoned, derelict sites) study, 148–151
background, 45–46
Boston's Dudley Street Neighborhood Initiative (DSNI) project, 52–54
Cleveland's Land Reutilization Authority (LRA) and Cleveland Land Bank project, 54–57
conclusions, 61–63
definitions, 47–48
list of interviewees, 78–79
methodology, 48–52
New York City, revitalization in, 57–58
Pittsburgh and the CRA, 58
project selection, 51–52
Providence, revitalization in, 58–60
quantitative or qualitative approach, 48–49
recommendations, 64–65
research goals, 47
Seattle, revitalization in, 60–61
success for whom, 50–51
web theory and defining success, 50

Underground Atlanta project, 26–28
U.S. Department of Housing and Urban Development (HUD), 7, 9, 46, 142
Upward Bound, 9
Urban Development Action Grants (UDAGs), 10, 81
Urban development literature, overview of, 4–12
Urban Land Institute, 8
Urban redevelopment, study on the impact of
age composition, 23–24
Atlanta example, 26–29
data used in measuring improvements, 22–26
educational levels, 25
future research directions, 42
housing units, occupied versus vacant, 26
income levels, 25–26
Minneapolis example, 30–32
neighborhoods used in study, 20–22
New Orleans example, 35–39
occupational composition, 24–25
Portland, Oregon example, 32–35
racial categories used, 23
results of study, 39–41
revitalization strategies, 20
Urban renewal
effects of, 8–9
programs, 7–8
Urban Revitalization: Policies and Programs (Wagner), 11–12

Vaughn, R., 10
Veterans' Administration (VA), 46

Wagner, F., 11
Warner, Sam Bass, 3
Washington, Robert, 62
Washington, D.C., 140
Weiss, Mike, 101
White, S., 11

Wolff, Barbara, 87, 95, 98
World Congress Center project,
    28–29

Yelder, Paul, 53–54